Cambridge Elements ≡

Elements in Publishing and Book Culture
edited by
Samantha Rayner
University College London
Rebecca Lyons
University of Bristol

CAPITAL LETTERS

The Economics of Academic Bookselling

J. M. Hawker
Blackwell Bookshop, Edinburgh

CAMBRIDGE
UNIVERSITY PRESS

CAMBRIDGE
UNIVERSITY PRESS

University Printing House, Cambridge CB2 8BS, United Kingdom

One Liberty Plaza, 20th Floor, New York, NY 10006, USA

477 Williamstown Road, Port Melbourne, VIC 3207, Australia

314–321, 3rd Floor, Plot 3, Splendor Forum, Jasola District Centre,
New Delhi – 110025, India

79 Anson Road, #06–04/06, Singapore 079906

Cambridge University Press is part of the University of Cambridge.

It furthers the University's mission by disseminating knowledge in the pursuit of
education, learning, and research at the highest international levels of excellence.

www.cambridge.org
Information on this title: www.cambridge.org/9781108717236
DOI: 10.1017/9781108675376

First published 2019

A catalogue record for this publication is available from the British Library.

ISBN 978-1-108-71723-6 Paperback
ISSN 2514-8524 (online)
ISSN 2514-8516 (print)

Capital Letters

The Economics of Academic Bookselling

Elements in Publishing and Book Culture

DOI: 10.1017/9781108675376

First published online: June 2019

J. M. Hawker

Blackwell Bookshop, Edinburgh

Author for correspondence: J. M. Hawker, jaki.hawker@blackwell.co.uk

ABSTRACT: Academic bookselling inhabits a landscape fundamentally impacted by legislative and political pressure, colonised by new textual forms and new publishing ventures, experiencing constant change. *Capital Letters* defines the academic bookshop, text, and market, examining change drivers in the UK, the United States and Asia. Drawing on current research, inclusive of commercial publishers and publishing interest groups, *Capital Letters* also includes quantitative and qualitative research data from academic booksellers. In evaluating the response of academic bookshops to the changing landscape, *Capital Letters* argues that academic booksellers can understand, shape, and lead a sustainable and equitable future for academic text within the marketplace.

KEYWORDS: academic bookselling, bookshops, retail, textbooks, publishing

ISBNs: 9781108717236 (PB), 9781108675376 (OC)

ISSNs:2514-8524 (online), 2514-8516 (print)

Contents

Introduction

In 2016–18 the Academic Book of the Future project coalesced academic interest in investigating the writing, publishing and selling of academic text. In looking to the future, the project also invoked contemporary stakeholders, drawing together teams of writers, publishers, librarians and booksellers. The *Gatherings* series of monographs builds on that collaboration, and as a contributing Element of *Gatherings*, *Capital Letters* interrogates the current ecology of academic bookselling. Throughout, *Capital Letters* establishes the premise that academic bookselling is heavily dependent on the marketplace, both exposed to and benefitting from market forces which include legislative and social influences as well as the individual financial decisions of textual consumers, and at the same time argues that academic booksellers have the capacity to understand, utilise and build on the transformative opportunities offered by that marketplace.

Capital Letters commences with a discussion of the definition of academic bookselling, and moves on to discuss the developing market within which the industry operates. With a primary focus on the United Kingdom, *Capital Letters* then discusses the increasing influence and opportunity of the worldwide marketplace for academic text, particularly in the second section of this Element, which covers pricing to that market. The third section covers the shifting ecology of the current marketplace in terms of market influencers, encompassing both external pressure and internal innovation. In the final section, *Capital Letters* examines the future of academic bookselling.

The Bookshop

In 1984, when Rachel Evans and Jack Meadows produced the monograph *Bookselling in Higher Education*, they confined their research to the campus bookshop; 'bookshops on, or very close to, the site of the institution' (Evans *et al.* 1984). In 2016, bookseller Craig Dadds stated in *The Academic Book of the Future*, 'Whatever form the academic book of the future predominately takes – whether virtual or physical – it is about providing options for our students and academics'(Lyons *et al.* 2016). The academic bookshop has become as fluid and inclusive as the text it purveys, bestriding both the

traditional local economy of the bricks-and-mortar bookshop and the world-wide technological marketplace. Today, the academic bookshop ranges from worldwide online providers to temporary site-specific pop-up bookstalls. It includes providers curating campus bookstalls (Kelvin Books); open access self-publishers working from their laptops (OpenIntro); established aggregators encompassing physical and digital text (Blackwell UK, John Smith's); EdTech companies which see themselves as online innovators rather than textual providers (Kortext, VitalSource); new economic models of text distribution from both established and new providers (New University Presses, academic-led presses, Knowledge Unlatched, Oxford University Press); and the many textual providers working through illegitimate distribution networks.

Yet the basic model of the academic bookshop remains, in both image and principle, the campus bookshop: a skills-based provider of academic text encompassing local representation, be that a physical presence on campus or branded digital provision.

The Market

The Booksellers Association lists 262 academic bookshops in the UK in 2018 (Campbell 2018), of which approximately 150 are chain bookshops with considerable online resources (John Smith's, Blackwell UK, and Waterstones) while the remainder are independent bookshops. Student survey responses in the UK (Hawker 2018h) indicate Amazon, Blackwell UK and John Smith's are the market leaders for online supply of physical text; digital text purchasers cite Amazon Kindle and CourseSmart (owned by VitalSource) as e-book sources for personal buyers. Digital chapter rental models are available in the UK for students (Benson-Armer 2014), but with the UK's lower textbook prices, postal-based physical rental models are yet to establish a market. Institutional purchasers of digital text, mediated by procurement frameworks, utilise market leaders VitalSource and Kortext, as well as library supplier platforms such as Dawsons. Individual academic publishers supply through both their own websites and platforms and/or through text aggregators. Individual writers can self-publish digital and/or physical text, with or without peer review, through a wide variety of sites. Legitimacy varies, and so

does the ability of a secondary supplier to access or distribute that text. Open access publishers provide text through their own platforms and/or adopt existing multiuser platforms. In addition to these legitimate sources, there are few digitised textbooks which are not available via torrent sites such as PirateBay, while pirated digital articles and monographs are concentrated on host sites such as SciHub and LibGen. Pirated physical text is available via the Amazon UK Marketplace (Hoffelder 2017) and other online bookshops (Stop Counterfeit Books 2017), as well as through local suppliers (Hawker 2018i).

The Academic Text

From this snapshot of academic text providers, it is clear that the nature of academic text has also changed. The archetypical academic book as seen from the academic bookshop is the student textbook, physical and/or digital, accounting for 56 per cent of 2017 sales at Blackwell Edinburgh, the second largest physical academic bookshop in the UK (Hawker 2018a). The basic form of the academic book from an institutional perspective, particularly for academic readers and writers in the humanities, remains the monograph (The Academic Book of the Future 2015). In terms of sales, the value metric of bookshop and publisher, monographs are seldom supplied to individual purchasers but rather to institutions, and thus for the bookshop the value and academic prestige of the monograph is considerably out-weighed by textbook provision to students. In production quantities, the journal article, a swift summary of research and a gateway to further publication, is by far the most common form of academic text. As a UK publication articles are now predominately digital and open access (Crossick 2015), and almost entirely supplied by the publisher (traditional or new) to institutional or personal purchaser.

Thus, for the academic bookshop the student textbook is their primary product, and it is on long-form, student-orientated text that *Capital Letters* will concentrate. The textbook itself, however, has developed since that initial 1984 report on the economics of academic bookselling to encompass digital text, physical/digital text, and the use of enhanced text and/or analytics. Textbooks have been deconstructed, with chapters alone increasingly cited as course reading and extracts utilised for flipped and blended

learning modules on VLEs (Virtual Learning Environments). With the addition of visible course notes, reviews and commentary online from author, course leaders and students, text has also become inclusive of ongoing interpretation, affirmation, correction and commentary. Accessing this enhanced and/or disarticulated digital text has meant not only new models of supply for established publishers, but new methods of publication from new digital providers, for whom content is only one of the many building blocks of EdTech. The academic 'book', as seen from the bookshop, is an inclusive and dynamic text: the successful academic bookshop has equally embraced innovation.

1 The Developing Marketplace

Within the current marketplace, academic booksellers currently face the dichotomies of increased demand for academic text and dire predictions for the state of the campus bookshop. Such uncertainty is not new: 'It may well be that we live in an epoch when the bookshop is an institution suspended between "the dying old society" and the "society struggling to be born." It has few defenders,' Edward Shils (Shils 1963); 'In the last few years, economic pressures have increased and times have become much harder for academic bookshops,' Rachel Evans and Jack Meadows (Evans *et al.* 1984); 'The move to digital and new forms of courseware will, however, make on-campus retailing uneconomic at some universities,' Peter Lake (Lake 2016b). 'Spotify for Books' e-book websites have come and gone with unnerving speed, and open access publishers have committed to libertarian ideals, argued for and against peer review and restructured funding models to encompass academic ideals and political patronage alongside content distribution. Traditional booksellers have moved online, and online booksellers have moved into the physical marketplace. EdTech includes academic text creators and compilers who do not define themselves as booksellers or publishers.

Change, for the academic bookshop, is the one defining feature of the marketplace. Yet that change is not ungoverned. There are quantifiable factors shaping the local and global market for academic text, and in examining those legislative and social drivers, the ways in which academic

booksellers have sought not only to respond to these challenges but to predict, shape and provide text for future readers can be discovered.

1.1 Market Values

In 2017, Bookmap valued the global book market as a whole at £122bn (Anderson 2017). Taking into account issues with recording the value of book sales, related to the changing definition of text and what constitutes a book in both academic and general markets (Kovač 2017), these figures are considered to be conservative (Williams 2017). The International Association for Scientific, Technical and Medical Publishers (STM) valued the total academic share of this market 'including journals, books, technical information and standards, databases and tools, and medical communications and some related areas' at $25.7 billion in 2017 (Johnson 2018): this figure, of course, only relates to STM titles. The International Publisher's Association pilot report of 2018, relating to the publishing industry of 2015–16, reveals some of the issues involved in collating global academic text sales: there are no figures available for 10 of the 35 countries surveyed (International Publisher's Association 2018). Despite the lack of ongoing statistical measurement, with 25 per cent of the world's population under fourteen years of age (The World Bank 2018) and many governments investing heavily in educational material (Williams 2018), the market is considered to be buoyant: Elsevier, currently the world's largest educational publisher, reported profits of £913m in 2017 (Matthews 2018).

In 2017, the Publisher's Association stated that academic and professional publishing sales in the United Kingdom were up 10 per cent on the previous year to £2.4bn. This figure is inclusive of digital academic and professional text, for which sales increased by 6 per cent to £277m (The Publisher's Association 2017). £1.3bn of these sales were processed through bookshops (excluding online bookshops): although 18 per cent of UK bookshops identify as academic bookshops (Centre for Economics and Business Research 2017), the sale of academic text is not restricted to those bookshops, so to state that campus bookshops alone achieved these sales would be inaccurate. The majority of academic text is sold through online bookshops, or by publishers direct to institutions. In 2005, for example, online sellers held an 11 per cent share of the overall UK retail

text market (The Bookseller's Association 2014): by 2014, this was 46 per cent (The Bookseller's Association 2017).

It is hard not to see the ongoing closures of academic bookshops on campus correlating with this market shift. For example, Plymouth University's Plymouth e-books project (Kavanagh 2015), commencing in 2011 and, by 2014, providing 4,062 students with 25,931 e-books sourced directly from publishers, corresponds with the closure of the Plymouth University Bookshop (Campbell 2016f). In total, eight academic bookshops closed between 2014 and 2017 (Campbell 2016e). Nielsen's Students' Information Sources in the Digital World 2015/16 reported that 72 per cent of students purchase course books from Amazon (Nielsen Book 2016). Yet 41 per cent of those same students had also purchased from a campus bookshop: Blackwell UK reported a 6 per cent profit increase in 2016–17, and after a 6 per cent drop in profits during 2015–16, John Smith's reported year-on-year results in 2016–17 and forecast additional confirmed income due in 2017–18. The marketplace remains buoyant for some academic booksellers.

1.2 Drivers

Yet book sales made at academic bookshops are not a simple transaction between customer and bookshop in an open marketplace. Consumer choice and effective bookshop management may be the apparent sales drivers, but legislative changes in the funding structure of research grants and student fees have a profound impact on the academic bookselling market, offering both incentives and barriers to textual provision through academic bookshops both on campus and online. This is particularly evident in the contrast between Scottish campus bookshops and those in the rest of the UK: both John Smith's and Blackwell have seen their Scottish bookshops consistently outperform equivalent stores in the rest of the UK, an ongoing model which is hard not to correlate with legislative differences in student funding. This legislation, directed at student and institution, has reshaped not only the marketplace of academia but the landscape of academic text.

1.2.1 Research Excellence Framework

Higher Education Funding Council for England (now UK Research & Innovation) Head of Research Policy Steven Hill created some controversy

within the book trade when discussing the next-but-one Research Excellence Framework process, beginning in 2021 but given the predicted title of REF 2027. REF, the Research Excellence Framework, covers funding for research at institutions in the same way that TEF covers teaching and learning (Office for Students 2017). Unlike TEF, REF covers the whole of the UK, with results being taken into account by the four separate funding bodies of England, Scotland, Ireland and Wales in determining research grants. The current REF has been instrumental in changing the ecology of journal text creation and distribution by requiring open access publication for funded research across the UK. Initiating body HEFCE (Higher Education Funding Council for England) stated:

> The core of the REF 2021 open access policy is that journal articles and conference proceedings must be available in an open access form to be eligible for the next REF. In practice, this means that these outputs must be uploaded to an institutional or subject repository. (Higher Education Funding Council for England 2016b)

This policy has led to major shifts in established publisher journal output, moving many UK-based journals to open access availability, but also ushering in the era of 'pay to publish' APCs (article processing charges) for academics and 'double-dipping' fees for libraries, who argued that they were paying subscription fees to access published material already funded by APCs (Research Libraries UK 2013). In addition, APCs themselves were often funded via an academic's host library. Publishers contested this argument. But with academic libraries already spending an estimated 72 per cent of their acquisition budget on journals and subscription services in 2017 (Publishers Communication Group 2017), up from 70 per cent in 2015, the cost of providing access to bundled journal articles is a considerable and controversial burden on libraries now also tasked with supporting TEF-related textual demands and, potentially, the development of new library-based publishing options (Pinfield *et al.* 2016).

While open access journal publishing has had little impact on academic bookshops – for most subscription services had moved to direct publisher

supply by 2012, when the OA Gold Standard came into force – REF 2027, as described by Steven Hill, will have an impact not only on academic publishers, but also on academic bookshops.

Speaking at the 2018 Redux University Press conference in February 2018 (University College London Press 2018), Steven Hill stated that monographs submitted for the REF 2027 process would need to be open access publications (Hill 2018b). This requirement had been discussed in the December 2016 Consultation on the second Research Excellence Framework (Higher Education Funding Council for England 2016a), but alongside an intention to 'move towards an open-access requirement for monographs' the consultation also acknowledged the need for flexibility and for exemptions. Hill did not discuss these issues in his speech, which created some controversy among conference attendees and later book trade commentators (Page 2018b). Immediate responses suggested views such as those of Bristol University Press publisher Alison Shaw, stating, 'We would happily publish open access, as long as we were confident that the revenue stream would come in.' Another anonymous publisher suggested this was a policy directed at 'decoupling the academic monograph from publishers', and 'an inexplicable direct attack on a thriving industry which fulfils the essential functions of development (through peer review), curation, dissemination and promotion' (Page 2018b). Academic publishers, holding an emergency IPG (Independent Publishers Guild) meeting in March 2018 (Page 2018a), argued that a requirement for monograph open access publishing, introducing APCs, would impact on early career academics; on those without well-resourced institutions, or without access to funding at all (Peter Clifford of Boydell and Brewer); on academics wishing to publish outside the UK in areas, such as the United States, without institutional open access publishing; and on universities forced to take money from research to fund publication (Sarah Caro of Princeton University Press).

While monograph sales to personal customers through bookshops are limited – and at any given moment less than 1 per cent of an academic bookshop's stock consists of monograph publications (Hawker 2018b), and those largely from local authors – academic bookshops do supply monographs to their academic libraries, particularly through procurement frameworks like APUC (Advanced Procurement for Universities and Colleges)

in Scotland and SUPAC (Southern Universities Purchasing Consortium) in England. If monograph production does become open access, funded through APCs, it is likely that (a) publication will retreat to digital production, as it has for journal articles, and (b) libraries will be asked to purchase monographs as bundles, as they do journals. These options exclude bookshops as physical text providers.

Even more disturbingly, REF 2027, in declaring all monograph publication open access, may have an impact on titles which border monograph and book, and academic and general audience. This category (Shapiro 1997) includes titles like the best-selling *Women & Power: A Manifesto*, by Mary Beard, the *Chicago Manual of Style*, or Rachel Carson's influential *Silent Spring*. 'Are they saying authors in the Humanities like Simon Schama and Mary Beard won't feature in the assessment of quality [because their trade publishers won't publish them open access]? Or are they saying we should give Mary Beard's books away? It is absurd,' said Ivon Asquith of Edinburgh University Press (Page 2018a). If, indeed, without the flexibility suggested by the Consultation on the second Research Excellence Framework, academic authors who receive funding through REF can only publish text as open access, then what happens to the academic bookshop, with the vast majority of its stock written by academic authors? Should the academic bookshop become nothing more than a repository of classics? Or, indeed, will the academic bookshop, with its mission to curate, disseminate, enable and gate keep, aid discovery and innovation and engage in outreach, become obsolete?

Steven Hill took the time to discuss publisher and bookseller queries in an interview for *The Bookseller* in March 2018 (Page 2018b). He promised consultation with academic publishers, and stated that the new models of REF 2027 are aimed at 'maximising the benefit of research findings by maximising the number of people who can access them' and the principle 'that the research, by and large, is funded out of public funds, and the idea that there are ethical arguments around the fact that it is not accessible to the people who funded it.' Hall added that the policy change, therefore, is because 'we are charged with spending taxpayers' money and making sure it is used as effectively as possible, and the push towards OA is driven by that,' whilst recognising that the scholarly publishing system 'needs to be

financially sustainable, so we need business models that enable people to operate'. It seems apparent from this interview that Hill was disconcerted by the level of resistance met by his policy statements, and by the anger at failure to communicate: his model appears very much drawn from short-form academic publishing, applied to long-form academic publishing without much recognition that the two are not built on the same structure in argument, in form, in funding or in distribution. Hill promises stakeholder consultation – 'opportunity for discussion and consultation and calls for evidence and all of that' – although, as with TEF, it appears inevitable that academic bookshops will be forced to adapt as best they can to a bookselling ecology profoundly influenced by the legislation of educational policy.

1.2.2 Teaching Excellence Framework and National Student Survey

Student tuition fees were introduced in 1998 and expanded after the publication of the Browne Report in 2010 to provide funding for institutions providing higher education. They are governed by the Teaching Excellence and Student Outcomes Framework (TEF). TEF 'recognises excellent teaching in UK higher education providers by rating them as gold, silver or bronze' (Office for Students 2016). The value of the TEF award indicates the monetary value of the tuition fee which the institution can assign to students, and thus the income available to the institution. As of 2018, 262 institutions across the UK participate in the TEF awards scheme, currently voluntary, although any institution registered with the Office for Students will be obliged to enter the next round of TEF assessments if they have more than 500 students attending courses. TEF participation in Scotland, where institutional funding is governed through the Quality Enhancement Framework (QEF) and Enhancement-led Institutional Review (ELIR), has been low, with only 5 of the 19 eligible institutions participating in TEF. English and EU undergraduate students studying in England, Scotland, Northern Ireland, or Wales currently face a maximum tuition fee of £9,250/annum: in Scotland, 'young students', defined as under twenty-five years of age, from Scotland or from the EU pay no tuition fees. Maintenance and hardship grants are available in all participating countries.

The Department for Education would argue that TEF recognises excellent teaching and provides a means for students to make an informed choice about which institution to attend (Office for Students 2016). However, metrics by which TEF is judged, and thus the value of the TEF award given to the institution, impacting directly on the institution's funding profile, could be argued to relate more to student experience and route to employment than to teaching excellence (Bagshaw 2017).

The 2016–17 metrics included results relating to teaching, assessment and feedback and academic support from the National Student Survey (NSS), to student retention, to leaver destination and employment and to the proportion of those leavers entering highly skilled employment.

The National Student Survey (NSS) results have been considered by the Department of Education to have had a disproportionate effect on TEF awards in 2017–18, and future NSS weightings will be halved (Department for Education 2017a). This is particularly relevant for academic booksellers, for it is these NSS student survey metrics which have had a considerable effect on textual provision within England, Wales and Northern Ireland, and are influencing textual provision in Scotland.

The NSS student survey, taken in the second semester of the academic year by students in their final year of study, contains 27 core questions and two open-ended questions, with additional optional questions designated by particular institutions (Office for Students 2018b). Learning resource–related questions 18, 19 and 20 have had an impact on academic bookshops:

18. The IT resources and facilities provided have supported my learning well.
19. The library resources (e.g. books, online services and learning spaces) have supported my learning well.
20. I have been able to access course-specific resources (e.g. equipment, facilities, software, collections) when I needed to.

Question 19, concerning learning resources, is particularly ironic as a metric of institutional performance, for the TEF framework itself (Department for Education 2017b) anecdotally only contains a reference to physical and digital learning resources, inclusive of academic text, as a result of lobbying by John Smith's Group Business Development Director

Peter Lake (Lake 2016b). Within the NSS framework, these questions imply that the educational institution is responsible for the management of physical and digital resources, and the ability of the student to access and effectively utilise those resources. Gold Award institutions indicate that '[o]utstanding physical and digital resources are actively and consistently used by students to enhance learning'; Silver Award institutions that '[h]igh quality physical and digital resources are used by students to enhance learning'; and Bronze Award Institutions that '[p]hysical and digital resources are used by students to further learning.'

1.2.3 Academic Administrators as Decision Makers

TEF standards, measured by the NSS response metrics, have led to a fundamental shift in academic bookselling, for in areas in the UK where tuition fees are governed by TEF, student use of resources – text – has become a metric with a measureable impact on institutional funding. In 2017, Gold Leaf produced the report *Resource Provision in Higher Education, Implications of the TEF and related initiatives* for the Academic Book Trade Conference 2017, studying changes in textual resource use and attitudes to resource use following the introduction of TEF (Bennett *et al.* 2017). Key stakeholders in resource use, university administrators, academics, librarians, students, publishers and booksellers were surveyed (100 selected participants) and interviewed (41 participants) and a student focus group was created for the report. 27 institutions were represented, with an even spread of interviewed participants from Russell Group, traditional non–Russell Group, post-1992 and newer universities. The majority of surveyed librarians came from post-1992 institutions, although otherwise the spread of responses was again even.

In terms of teaching and learning materials needed to fulfil the requirements of TEF, university administrators universally agreed that more electronic resources would be used. They 'often mentioned these within the content of "blended learning" or material produced by the university itself, such as recorded lectures and the products of "flipped learning". Some made it clear that student opinion of learning resources would be closely monitored.' Twelve of fourteen publishers said that TEF would alter their approach to new product development, with some adding that

their marketing strategy would also change. Those changes would include less reliance on US editions of books, development of tests and assessment suites and supplementary texts (enhanced text), setting up pilot projects, mapping products to learning objectives and 'better communication'. This last is a constant for all participants in all areas. All surveyed stakeholders were in agreement that interactive learning resources would play a bigger role – although opinions differed on micro content and/or custom content: 41 per cent of librarians thought this would be needed, but only 22 per cent of academics thought so.

Encouragingly for the academic publishing industry, all but one of the university administrators believed there was still a strong role for textbooks. Innovations which were favoured included e-books (approximately half of university administrators thought these would become more used than printed books), open access textbooks, deconstructed chapter access and text extracts. Only three of the librarians interviewed believed textbooks were crucial, while others believed research-led resources, journal articles and other sources of information were more important. Librarians were also uneasy about the costs involved in supplying textbooks, with only one librarian confident about their ability to supply textbooks, 'because students were still expected to buy their own'. Eighty-six per cent of publishers interviewed were confident about the continuing role of textbooks, albeit evolving in format: 100 per cent of booksellers thought the same.

The role of the bookshop, however, was less favoured. Of the administrators, only a quarter thought the academic bookshop has a future, although this response was split between those universities which did have a bookshop and those which did not: by chance the majority did not work in an institution which had a bookshop. Those administrators who did not support bookshops said 'it was important and valuable for students to buy books, but that they were most likely to buy from Amazon'. Librarians, from the same institutions, were much more upbeat, with only one suggesting the bookshop has no future. Publishers were more equivocal, with 71 per cent stating that 'the campus bookshops play an important role in the ecosystem and that there is a future for them' while by an almost unanimous majority advocating new business models, described above, which exclude the bookshop from campus textbook provision. All of the booksellers

except one believed they had a robust future. It is notable that those respondents closest to students in terms of ongoing textual use – librarians and booksellers – were the respondents who felt that there was a continuing need for a campus bookshop.

To achieve the 'Outstanding physical and digital resources' (TEF) and the 'library resources (e.g. books, online services and learning spaces) [which] have supported my learning well' (NSS) spurring the *Resource Provision in Higher Education* report, institutions have adopted a number of different models, often piloted at school or department level. As of yet, no UK university has adopted an institution-wide solution to text supply to students, although some have come close with bursary cards or e-books for all student enrollees, so the visibility of many projects is limited to stakeholders, student participants and researchers.

1.2.4 Investment in Learning Resources

Investment in learning resources has been explicitly linked to TEF. For example, Matthew Lawson of Library & Student Support at Middlesex University argues that '[t]he university's relative position in league tables and NSS ranking provided an incentive for the Executive to consider investing in the library.' He proposed successfully that the library was 'comparatively underfunded in terms of learning materials budgets and that this was impacting negatively on student satisfaction', achieving as a result funding for 24/7 opening, enhanced printing facilities for students and extra resources, and concluded that 'these improvements appear to have had a positive impact on both informal and formal measures of student satisfaction and to have contributed to the university rising up the league tables' (Lawson 2015).

Lawson goes on to discuss the 'free e-books for all' projects – the supply of digital textbooks through John Smith's and Kortext, firstly as a pilot project, and then to all students. His argument for so doing explicitly references TEF and the NSS as well as enhancing teaching and learning. The main arguments Lawson gave for supporting the scheme were as follows:

(i) to support the university's strategy of 'enhancing student achievement and satisfaction'
(ii) to improve NSS results

(iii) to provide an additional means of attracting students to the university
(iv) to demonstrate value for money in the face of higher tuition fees
 (v) to assist with course delivery, in that lecturers would be sure all their students have the essential text
(vi) to enhance pedagogy through the ability to annotate passages and share notes.

It is important to note that while much of the institutional investment, such as that of Middlesex University, around text acquisition and usage does relate to the TEF metrics, the majority builds on previous pre-TEF research and projects centred around text use, often on those projects seeking to cut back on text cost to the institution and to the institution's students prior to the TEF implementation. Nevertheless, TEF has led to an ongoing reassessment of institutional text use, manifesting in both expected and unexpected results.

1.2.5 No Hidden Fees

The highest profile change to institutional text use has been the 'no hidden fees' course, an attractive advertisement to students paying tuition fees. Such courses include any required learning resources, physical and/or digital text, which can be provided via a number of different methods and for some students, in a number of different formats.

Digital text-based learning resources are likely to be provided through or embedded within a VLE, often specific to a single course. Material may be produced by the university and directly embedded into the VLE (see, for example, Sandy Britain and Oleg Liber's much-cited assessment of VLEs (Britain *et al.* 1999), *A Framework for Pedagogical Evaluation of Virtual Learning Environments*, which envisages all learning materials being available through the VLE) or provided by an external supplier and wrapped within the VLE; see, for example, VitalSource's consequent claim (Kim 2017) to be the biggest supplier of digital textbooks in the world. Where such integration is not possible due to the nature of the text involved, the university may supply the necessary software and hardware to a student: for example, the University of Westminster's Mobile Learning project (#FSTMobileLearning) has been running for three years and supplies

2,000 students a year with an iPad along with course materials, creating a paperless learning environment for STEM students (University of Westminster 2015). Notably, this project is supplied by Apple specialist Academia for Education rather than a traditional digital coursebook supplier like VitalSource, Kortext or a single publisher: academic text forms only a small part of what is thought to constitute a complete teaching environment (Chuck 2017).

Other universities have supplied single books rather than integrating text into a VLE or learning app: for example, Plymouth University's e-book project, which supplies e-book files to undergraduate students, offers lecturer-specified text(s) for a subject area regardless of format so long as that text is digitised. In this case, project leaders chose not to align with any proprietary platform. Nonaligned projects offer the potential of choice which aligned projects do not: for example, in 2016 the University of Edinburgh Business School moved to supplying on-campus MBA students with digital text through Kortext. Student feedback suggested that access to digital text alone was an option unfavourably viewed by students. In consequence, the School also supplies physical text via Kortext, the latter collaborating with local booksellers to do so (Hawker 2018e).

No-fees-added courses can be intersectional. For example, Andrew Barker, the librarian at the University of Liverpool, working with the University of Liverpool Press, has been leading a JISC-sponsored textbook through the *institution as e-book creator* initiative. The first book produced was for a Financial Management module, required by 900 distance learners. An open access custom book, it is available in both physical and digital options, integrated into a VLE, supported by institutional funding for both production and supply (Barker 2015). Barker does not mention costs, but a similar 2004 project at the Liverpool Business School was funded at £30,000 (Kidd 2010) and the eight-book *institution as e-book creator* project is funded at '£250 k to £1 m' or £31,250 – £125,000 per title published (JISC 2015). At point of purchase, assuming a 33 per cent margin and no discount, that level of funding equates to a recommended retail price (RRP) of £51.99 – £207.99. For reference, the cost to students of the Financial Management textbook replaced by the Liverpool e-book project, in 2016, was RRP £56 apiece, or £50,400 in total.

No-fees-added courses, particularly in England, Scotland and Wales, remain a popular and emotive choice for students: the Gold Leaf student focus group, for example, argued that no student should have to pay for course materials, while student unions across the UK have supported inclusive courses. Leeds Beckett University students argued in January 2018 that with students spending between £100 and £199.99 on course materials in their first semester, and with 20 per cent of their additional course outlay being spent on textbooks along with additional costs, the University should pursue a 'No More Hidden Fees' policy (Leeds Beckett Student Union 2018).

1.2.6 Equitable Access

It is no accident that traditional and digital content publishers have leaned heavily on the 'inclusive' nature of digital educational provision. For publishers like Pearson supporting research into global equity within higher education, 'access means more than entry and participation; it also means completion of a high quality programme' (Pearson Publishing Ltd 2017a), summarising their sponsored report, *Charting Equity in Higher Education: Drawing the Global Access Map* (Atherton *et al.* 2017). Pearson claims to 'help people make progress in their lives through learning' through the company's platforms, assessments and services, as well as through investment in digital curriculum–based Affordable Private Education Center, Inc. or APEC Schools. These low-cost and/or voucher-supported private and charter schools, which allow Pearson full resource and curriculum control and are often supported through public educational funding, have been criticised by teachers unions for 'essentially ensuring that a large number of the world's most vulnerable children have no hope of receiving free, quality education', while the UN too called for greater oversight of associated education providers (Kamenetz 2016). Stating that 'students are the primary focus of everything we do at Cengage', Cengage launched Cengage Unlimited, an all-access pass to Cengage's digital content, in 2016. Fernando Bleichmar, EVP and Chief Product Officer, said, 'Knowing that cost is among the highest hurdles facing students, we embarked on a very deliberate path to find a solution' (Searchlight 2017). The service is available for, in 2018, $119.99 per term or $179.99 per year, allowing access to 22 K+ digital products.

To put these investments in context, Pearson issued five profit warnings in the four years up to and including 2017. Cengage restructured in July 2013; they were $5.8 billion in debt. For Pearson, the aggregate profit from government-partnered private education, alongside a captive test group for experimental programming, makes APEC schools attractive to shareholders, while for Cengage, confronted with students purchasing second-hand, rental or no books, a guaranteed $179.99/year/student income is considerably greater than that received from the estimated 25 per cent of US students purchasing new textbooks. As academic Rajiv Jhangiani states, 'Just how inclusive are "inclusive access" e-textbook programs? . . . It is little wonder (although rather amusing) that the large commercial publishers have sought to repaint themselves as the saviours of those suffering at the hands of their own business model.' He points out, given the restricted access of provider-owned platforms, that 'the true power of open access comes not from a resource being free of cost but rather from the freedoms to reuse, retain, redistribute, revise, and remix content' (Jhangiani 2017). For Jhangiani, as for many academics concerned with the provision of academic textbooks, open access publishing is a choice in which the morality of equitable access encompasses content supplier as well as content consumer. As Nicole Allen, director of open education for the Scholarly Publishing and Academic Resources Coalition, points out, the very term inclusive access is a misnomer: 'It is the opposite of inclusive, because it is premised on publishers controlling when, where and for how long students have access to their materials, and denying access unless they pay for it' (McKenzie 2017).

For some universities, therefore, the solution to equitable access has been a bursary grant to cover costs, redeemable against options including textbooks, stationery, printing costs, cafeteria or student union shop expenses, accommodation, transport and/or childcare. Bursaries vary in value, format and conditions, but the most common application has been through a card-based purse of funds. In some cases, the student can choose their options, and in others spending is pre-allocated. The University of East London, for example, pioneering bursary cards in 2007, partnered with campus bookseller John Smith's for predetermined textbook spending. Students responded positively. However, bursary cards have been an

administrative headache for institutions, with students spending funds outside predicted options, and some outlets expanding their range of products in order to attract those funds. Bookseller John Smith's offers tents, clothing and homeware through its online store, and the Manchester Metropolitan University's Metcard users spent so heavily on audio and computer equipment via the campus Blackwell Bookshop bursary that conditions had to be redrawn (Hawker 2017a). Administrators for some cards began to demand itemised student-purchased product lists from suppliers, and others, including the University of East London and Queen's University, Belfast, withdrew the bursary card altogether.

1.3 Managing Decision Making

From the summary above, it is notable that decision making related to textbook selection and provision within the academic community has shifted. For many years, a text was selected by a course leader and that choice was conveyed to publisher, library, bookshop and student; the choice of format and supplier belonged to the student. While this is still the majority decision-making model in Scotland, for the rest of the UK, decision making has shifted from course leaders to administrators. In some cases, librarians have seized the opportunity to administrate textbook choices, utilising reading list aggregators like Talis or Leganto, securing budgets to supply textbooks to students or venturing into publishing themselves. In other institutions, library staff are 'not all interested in "mission creep to become publishers"' (Adema *et al.* 2016), and course leaders have retained both budget and choice relating to textbook supply. For many institutions, decision making has been moved to departmental head or vice-principal level or above.

For the academic bookshop this decision-making shift has meant a change in strategy, as some lines of communication close down and others open. What has been a universal experience, however, is that communication needs to be open and inclusive: libraries, for example, have little access to physical copy purchase rates, so they may be caught out when students argue for physical copy. Librarians, informed by demand-led text ordering, generally have a clearer image of research and teaching trends. Equally, bookshops are often well informed about custom text, physical text use and study skills

issues, as they watch students making text-based financial choices. Both can work together with faculty to enable student choice. Yet it is particularly notable that the further a decision maker is from contact with students, the less weight is given to the value of an academic bookshop (Bennett & Bennett 2017), and the less likely it is that administrators see benefits to academics and students in involving booksellers in textual provision. This is particularly noticeable in the history of bookshop closures. While financial pressures have caused some closures, others have been the result of administrative decisions; for example, the closures of the independent Queen's University and Blackwell Heriot Watt campus bookshops were managerial choices which were both protested by faculty to no avail.

Strategies vary for managing changes in decision making. Blackwell, for example, depended heavily on campus-based bookshop managers pursuing their own contacts in order to secure institutional funding from decision makers for physical or digital text, while John Smith's was swift to create a dedicated UK-wide sales team. For independent academic bookshops, strategic partnerships with publishers and institutions have successfully negotiated this new landscape. For all academic bookshops, the swiftness of change, not just in terms of decision making but inclusive of new forms of text, has been both an opportunity and a struggle: intensive training, for example, has been needed for some booksellers to be able to provide student support for digital as well as physical text. At the same time oversight of the bookshop's access to student response has been useful for academic decision makers. For example, when Blackwell Edinburgh found that 36 per cent of first year chemistry students were purchasing physical copy in addition to the digital text they were provided through their VLE via institutional purchase, school administrators redirected funds. For first-year biology students, though, low take-up of a text seen as vital to the course resulted in both a change of title and a shift to both physical and digital institutional purchase.

1.4 Bookseller Response

Some academic bookshops are already working towards the future of academic text in the era of TEF and REF 2027. Movers and shakers within the industry have responded to this new bookselling ecology in very

different ways, and the strategy taken by the two major academic bookshop chains within the UK, John Smith's and Blackwell UK, illustrates this divide.

1.4.1 John Smith's Aspire

John Smith's moved early and forcefully into two areas of academic text provision: institutional digital text provision (Aspire Connect, first used by Anglia Ruskin, in 2012), and institutional grant or bursary funds earmarked for textbooks delivered through a card scheme or through direct textbook provision (Aspire Engage). Both options are directly linked to TEF and consequent investment in learning resources. 'With the introduction of higher fees and TEF ... [universities] ... are now investing even more in learning resources that support student research and study' (JS Group 2018).

Aspire 'is the mostly widely adopted and used cashless bursary solution in the UK Higher Education sector' (Wood 2017). It currently covers fourteen institutions, the majority post-1992 institutions without a bookshop on campus, for whom the no-hidden-fees and direct funding options provide an additional incentive to attract students. The York St John University Aspire card, for example, offers first-year students £100, 'used to purchase items that will help with learning on your course for example books and other course materials pre-determined by Subject Directors' (JS Group 2017). The University of Chester offers 'a package of essential textbooks for your undergraduate course chosen by your programme leader' (University of Chester 2017). It is notable that these schemes as advertised to students are characterised as helping with studies, while to university administrators John Smith's advertises that '[u]niversities that have introduced Aspire Engage have seen their NSS results improve at almost twice the national average'. 'Aspire solutions can enrich the student experience', they claim, and 'there is data from Aspire solutions that shows a positive correlation between student engagement with learning resources and progression and final degree outcomes' (JS Group 2017). These are, of course, TEF metrics.

Recognising the considerable investment required to develop a digital text platform, John Smith's instead partnered with Kortext to offer both

direct digital and mixed option digital/physical text provision to students. This is both a shared supply model, where John Smith's supplies any physical text needed, and Kortext supplies platform, analytics and text, digital customer support, and any development work required to integrate with an institution's VLE, and a profit share model, where any contracts gained by Kortext and John Smith's working together are mutually beneficial. It may appear as if John Smith's has made a better deal in this partnership, but Kortext states of this partnership, as they have later of their Blackwell UK partnership, that it is to Kortext's advantage to align themselves with the excellent reputation, skills, and local institutional knowledge of their longer-established partner (Frost 2015). Mirroring Kortext, Aspire Connect is marketed as an analytics tool – 'Aspire Connect will source your resources, will deliver them directly to your students, will drive usage and engagement and provide data and analytics on that usage and engagement.' (JS Group 2018).

Aspire is a successful commercial programme. Of the bookseller's 2015 turnover, £40.66m, with operating profit of £336,000, Peter Gray, chairman and C.E.O. of John Smith's parent company, the JS Group, stated, 'the Aspire bursary platform had been the main driver behind the company's growth' (Cowdrey 2017). The year 2018 saw the company state that 'recurring Aspire revenues based on long-term contracts now account for 75 percent of its UK HE revenues' (Campbell 2018). In 2016, Peter Lake stated that 'the emphasis for booksellers will shift to providing services, software and solutions to universities'. He sees the company realigning towards investment in and development of learning resources management services, digital content delivery platforms and data analytic services. He also acknowledges the need for collaboration: 'booksellers are well placed to work with universities on the selection of resources' (Lyons *et al.* 2016).

Interestingly, in analysing the Aspire programme in 2015, researcher Simon Frost links the programme not just with 'a sustainability unusual in an age when many booksellers regard themselves as endangered species', but with an epistemological stance: 'in an age of dominant neo-liberal capitalism, what is indispensable is a text delivery system that is effective, if any belief in the emancipatory potential of higher education is to remain viable.' Frost goes on to characterise John Smith's operations as 'arranged to increase the widest range of gains available through education material supply for the

greatest number of participants', naming readers, students, teachers and educators, student-support teams and university executive management. Usefully, he describes John Smith's as a bookseller which perceives itself as having 'a core business in academic textbooks, but a main activity in problem-solving for HEIs, which includes helping institutions to reach target objectives'. Frost argues that the key benefits the bookseller offers in the process of integrating with an organisation and moving towards target objectives are knowledge, particularly of text, courses and lecturers, learning styles, student purchase and use patterns, publisher negotiation – notably in the production of custom text – and a history of collaboration with all stakeholders. It is also interesting to note at this stage Frost's assessment of the John Smith's campus shops. His data is drawn from shop manager interviews between September 2014 and February 2015. Frost states:

> The campus shop gives JS a presence that online services and branded imagery alone cannot provide. Relationships with key reps can be developed; staff may come in to browse; explanations for anomalies in low penetration rates can be gathered more readily (hearing that the lecturer is on a research leave); and the doors on which managers knock in search of reading lists are always nearby. Since bursaries change from year to year, sometimes significantly, shop managers and regional and business managers can liaise on the information they gather from lecturer and VC-level contacts. Proximity makes it easier to pick up indications of changes in policy, fortune favouring the well-prepared visit, and word-of-mouth is instrumental in increasing the take-up of ASPIRE. But above all, unlike online provision, the bookshop has the clear potential benefit for students by becoming a welcoming refuge. (Frost 2015)

1.4.2 Additional Strategy

Together with the positive delivery of Aspire, John Smith's also reassessed their delivery of physical text through campus bookshops, despite the

positive views expressed by managers in Frost's survey. Alongside many other booksellers, financial constraints meant that in the last decade John Smith's was forced to retreat from a number of campuses. Peter Lake argues that 'the textbook may be less relevant in the future', and that the student retail model of the on-campus bookshop 'will persist and change as a broader range of goods and services will be offered to students' (Lyons *et al.* 2016). At the Future Space of Bookselling conference in 2016, Lake said that he would not be surprised if the John Smith's of the future had no on-campus bookshops at all, servicing universities through online and off-site provision of platform-based learning resources. At that point in time, he stated, half the product lines in John Smith's campus bookshops were not text based, a provision reflected on the John Smith's website. Frost (2015) argues that these non-book products are 'part of the solution' equipping students with items they need to 'enter HEI, stay the course and exit to a job' – hence, 'the Amazon-competitive prices to attract students, the bicycles to help them get to university and the interview suits.'

Company reports show a continuing revenue stream from physical text as well as digital, and from single customers as well as institutions. In 2016, when revenue dropped to £38.1m, 'overall numbers of students served by Aspire schemes also declined, and the company said there had been a "planned de-emphasis of lower margin products"'. But 'the company saw a 75% surge in e-book sales, with e-books now representing 17% of all book sales', and 'books sales rallied showing growth of 4.5%, with books as a category accounting for 56% of sales up from 49% in the prior year' (Cowdrey 2017a). The year 2017 saw some improvement, as revenue was 'flat year-on-year at £38.2 m for the year', and operating profit 'increased to £1.5 m from £0.8 m'. Three new institutions enrolled with Aspire; four additional institutions enrolled with Aspire pilot projects. David Marshall, group commercial director, stated that 'growth is being driven by two primary factors – the growth in Aspire contracts where online is often the primary or sole channel and in addition general market changes in student purchasing preferences, with more students choosing to source content and course materials online as opposed to in a physical store' (Campbell, 2018).

John Smith's solution-based commercial strategy, concentrating on institutional provision of learning resources, often digital, while for the time

being retaining some campus bookshops as providers of additional student-focused products, is currently profitable and sustainable. In conversation, Peter Lake remarked that John Smith's, as a public limited company, had to innovate to succeed – unlike Blackwell UK, a privately owned institution (Hawker 2016a).

1.4.3 Blackwell Learning

Blackwell UK took a different route to the challenges of TEF. Another long-established academic bookseller, Blackwell UK is privately owned by Toby Blackwell, who is prepared to invest in capital-intensive projects for both academic and general customers. As a result, Blackwell too followed a dual strategy, investing in the digital platform Blackwell Learning, launched in September 2015, and in the value-based physical text offer 'Student Price Match Guarantee'. In addition, Blackwell invested in their online offer to general customers, developing logistical support, expanding marketplaces and utilising targeted discounting.

The bookshop's digital platform Blackwell Learning was effectively an online digital text aggregator, intended for use by institutions providing digital text to students. Development work was undertaken with two main aims: to prioritise the student journey through text in the visible interface, and to protect publisher rights. Blackwell Learning's selling points to universities as a digital text platform were therefore the protection of copyright, and the prioritising of the student experience, along with a suite of accessible and adaptable text features. The site was VLE compatible depending on development work. Unlike Kortext's platform, Blackwell Learning did not offer analytics: unlike CourseSmart, it did not offer rental models or chapter downloads, although any suitable file could be ingested into the platform and at least one custom book was offered. Blackwell Learning was open to individual customers as well as to institutions, and the site offered perpetual access to text once purchased, in contrast to many publisher-specific institutional digital text offers.

Blackwell Learning was well-received within the bookselling industry, winning the Innovation Prize at the annual trade Academic, Professional and Specialist Awards in March 2016 (Campbell 2016a). However, take-up across the higher educational community was slow, and it became apparent

that considerable development work was required to align the platform with institutional IT systems. User experience was impacted by some incompatibility with some personal devices. In December 2017, the platform was sold to Kortext for an unknown sum, the two companies entering into a digital text provider partnership at the same time, much as Kortext had previously done with John Smith's (Campbell 2016c). In working with educational technology, Blackwell UK had come to the conclusion that collaboration was the best option for the company. Kortext was optimistic about their new partner, with owner James Gray stating that the company was determined 'to work in partnership with the education sector to provide the broadest access to digital learning resources and the best student experience in using those resources', and that 'Blackwell's has an outstanding academic reputation . . . and we are excited to partner with them during this time of incredible change in education.' Blackwell CEO David Prescott said, 'We believe that we are best able to achieve this by partnering with Kortext rather than continuing to invest in a separate platform. Alongside our shops, our ecommerce platform and our strong corporate and institutional relationships, this new partnership will help us provide the best solutions and service to our customers as they transition from print to digital usage as part of everyday learning.'

At this point it is too early to judge if the Blackwell/Kortext partnership will prove as sustainable as the John Smith's/Kortext partnership, but with two collaborative projects started as the partnership came into force in January 2018 and more to follow, both partners are optimistic (Hawker 2018e). It is particularly notable, in favour of success, that Blackwell has campus shops in the pre-1992 and Russell Group universities where both Kortext and bursary provision for student purchase have yet to make inroads.

1.4.4 Additional Strategy

Blackwell's product specific TEF-related strategy was far more successful. Introduced in the second semester of 2015, 'Student Price Match Guarantee' promotes individual student purchase of physical textbooks, assuming that (a) universities will continue to request that students make individual textbook purchases and that (b) students and other customers will continue

to purchase physical text for personal use, both issues of some discussion within the trade. Nevertheless, the strategy was put into practice. The price match guarantees that Blackwell will offer textbooks to students (and indeed any other customer) at a price the same as or cheaper than online competitors, namely Amazon. The strategy is marketed aggressively on campus, taking advantage of local contacts: a swift check online reveals blog posts from, for example, the University of Nottingham (2017), University of Sheffield (2017), and the University of Kent (2017), and online on the company's website. As an offer, Student Price Match Guarantee has been remarkably successful, increasing sales in-store and online (Hawker 2018g).

Student Price Match Guarantee did meet some internal dissent, for managers were wary about cutting into the already thin margin on academic books. However, a post-introduction analysis by Darrell Thrush-Denning and Jaki Hawker of the Blackwell South Bridge store indicated that the profit margin lost through Student Price Match Guarantee was in fact marginally less in total than previous margin loss due to aggressive discounting, visible in 2016 comparisons to 2015 and 2014 (Thrush-Denning *et al.* 2016).

Blackwell added to these offers by heavy investment in their overall online capacity and with additional resource for new bookshops, detailed below, and this must be taken into account when considering company financial reports. Nevertheless, in 2015 bookshop sales were up 2.9 per cent with CEO David Prescott commenting that the success supports 'the decision to focus on a combined strategy of its physical shops and online presence' (Campbell 2017a). While bookshop sales in 2016 'were flat on a like-for-like basis' with major contributor Manchester consigned to portable cabins during long-term university building work, by 2017 the strategy had really begun to pay off, as sales surged by 12 per cent. 'The strong top line growth was largely attributable to Blackwell's expanding online operations, together with solid results from its retail portfolio of academic and flagship shops. All shops reported positive contributions during the year,' commented David Prescott. Reflecting the company's commitment to a general as well as academic strategy, Prescott said 'we are moving the business towards a multichannel approach and have invested in e-commerce. We are trying to remove the barriers between the shops and online' (Campbell 2018).

Anecdotally, meeting at the APS conference in 2015, JS Group Business Development Director Peter Lake remarked on the Student Price Match Guarantee physical book strategy to Blackwell CEO David Prescott, citing John Smith's investment in the potential of institutionally purchased digital text. When meeting again in 2016, Lake mentioned this exchange, noting the value of continuing to invest in physical text as well as digital (Hawker 2017b).

1.4.5 Independent Bookseller Response

Chain bookseller responses to legislation-related institutional investment in learning resources involve major commitments of capital and resources beyond the reach of a single academic bookstore, the majority of bookshops identifying as academic bookshops. What, then, are the TEF-related solutions for an independent campus bookshop?

For successful independent bookshops, the answer lies in embedding themselves within their parent institution and community. Craig Dadds of the Canterbury Christ Church University bookshop comments, 'We need to do more than roll with the times – we need to take charge and create opportunities. And we will do this by working together with not just publishers and librarians – but with our lecturers, as colleagues and authors, and with our students and customers' (Lyons *et al.* 2016). The Word, of Goldsmiths College, University of London, has committed to 'working in a collaborative relationship with the university, closely liaising with teaching staff and responding to students' needs,' and providing 'a welcoming and attractive environment that both reflects and enhances the learning experience'.

Popular strategies include supporting sustainable second-hand text collection and resale, either through direct purchase as at The Word or through facilitating sales for the original text owner, taking a percentage of the purchase price on sale. Emulating chain bookstores, some campus stores offer student reward schemes. The Word, for example, offers a £5 voucher for every £100 spent. Others emphasise local knowledge. Appleseed offers a reading list database and a print shop alongside traditional campus bookshop lines – official university branded apparel and gifts printed by Appleseed.

That theme of embedding within the local academic community is picked up by University of Westminster bookshop Marylebone Books Ltd, which provides 'a comprehensive service for students, teaching staff and the campus libraries'. Marylebone Books Ltd makes a point of stating that they employ students, and offers opportunities for feedback. It is also clearly affiliated to the university, hosting links to the library and to the university's VLE, Blackboard. Warwick University's bookshop is renowned in the trade for stock knowledge and reading list support, essential for student trust and teaching support.

Other bookshops have embraced their local community as a whole. No Alibis, in Belfast, bills itself as a crime bookstore which also serves students at Queen's University. Next-day orders, merchandise, student discounts and eccentric reading list collation, along with an energetic programme of local author and band events, make this one of the most vibrant and unusual academic bookshops in the UK.

For most successful independents, all of these options and more contribute to an integrated textual service. In discussion, Chris Dadds notes that the Canterbury Christ Church University bookshop offers speedy replenishment of stock as well as next-day customer orders, discounts, custom texts and book bundles, rare book searches, engagement with open days and graduation days, author events and conferences and carefully selected student employees. 'It isn't just about selling books, it is about meeting customer needs and providing our students with options when meeting customer needs and providing our students with options when it comes to accessing information and acquiring knowledge, whether that is an e-book, a second-hand purchase, or borrowing a title from the university library' (Lyons *et al.* 2016).

Perhaps the only option UK academic bookshops do not generally offer is the renting of academic textbooks common to US campus stores with their higher textbook pricing, although Blackwell did provide a trial offer in 2014.

Yet sometimes even the passion and hard work of an academic bookseller is not enough when set against the decisions taken by their host university. Dan Johns of Plymouth University Bookshop discusses the negative impact of the low profit margins endemic to academic bookselling:

'we were finding it impossible to run a bookshop on 30% discount from publishers,' and of decisions by the University, 'we had a breakthrough with Plymouth University when it gave its students an electronic card to spend money in our shop, but the institution found it was cheaper to buy e-books for the students directly from publishers, so that's what it did.' The bookshop closed in December 2015 (Campbell 2016f).

Some new academic bookshops, however, are opening, with investment and innovation firmly rooted in both digital and physical textual provision. Blackwell's new Liverpool University branch is one of the chain's New Academic Bookshops. Investment for these model shops lies in digital flexibility, with interactive touch screen databases for customers, 24-hour supply chain management and in-store digital book access. Design is centred on study spaces rather than bookshelves, and staff are focused around customer service rather than stock management. Cafes are essential. The company began investment in this new model with two bookshops, Cardiff and Liverpool, and will reopen Belfast and Manchester in 2019 as customer-orientated, digitally enabled spaces, showing a confidence in the future despite – or perhaps alongside – the impact of TEF and REF (Campbell 2016d).

1.5 Impact of Brexit

Brexit and its associated policy change are already having an impact on the academic bookshop. Some challenges are unique to bookshops; others affect the whole academic community.

For Blackwell South Bridge Foreign Language Buyer Rebecca Heitsch, the immediate financial impact of the vote was seen in the cost to the shop of imported titles. The fall of the pound against the euro and the dollar led to price hikes of 15 to 20 per cent. Postage charges from the EU also saw a considerable increase. 'I can't absorb these costs into the current book price,' Rebecca stated. The rising costs of UK distribution have not only impacted on the selling price of foreign language titles, but on publishers seeking to maintain their presence in the open market of the European Union, directly influencing, for example, Pearson's decision to shift their distribution centre from the UK to Belgium, and Springer's decision to distribute Palgrave titles from their distribution hub in Heidelberg,

Germany. With delivery from Pearson currently averaging eight working days ('We aim to deliver within 2–3 working days of receipt of your order,' Pearson Publishing Ltd 2017b), and from Springer, ten (Hawker 2018i), this Brexit-related distribution issue will impact heavily on academic bookshops relying on speedy stock replenishment during the vital first- and second-semester periods, and on rapid customer order delivery throughout. It is hard not to envisage a growing reliance on swift UK-based wholesaler delivery rather than direct publisher sales for bookshops dependent on rapid delivery to retain customers.

This concern assumes students on campus buying books. In 1984, Evans and Meadows observe, 'the number of overseas students in the UK has fallen because of the rapid rise in overseas students' fees. Since such students tend to buy more books on average, their loss has a disproportionate effect on bookshop sales (Evans *et al.* 1984). In 2016, a student survey at Blackwell South Bridge revealed that 35 per cent of student customers were overseas students, a number proportionally higher than the then 25 per cent of overseas students within the Edinburgh student body (Hawker 2016c). Any drop in overseas student numbers could, therefore, disproportionately affect bookshop income.

An initial survey by the think tank Higher Education Policy Institute (Conlon *et al.* 2017) suggested that for UK-based university courses 'some changes (e.g. higher fees for EU students) would reduce demand. Others (e.g. depreciation of sterling) would increase demand by reducing the price of studying in the UK for those from other countries'. On balance, the report argues, 'harmonising the rules for EU and non-EU students could reduce enrolments from other EU countries by over 31,000 students (a 57% decline in EU students)' while 'a 10% depreciation of sterling could increase enrolments from all other countries by around 20,000 students – an increase of 9%'. In addition, 'the Home Office has [also] promised to consult on making it harder for international students to come and study in the UK. This puts all the positive effects of current global changes at risk while doing nothing to ease the negative effects. If the extra 20,000 students a year who are expected to come to the UK as a result of the depreciation of sterling were not allowed to come, then they could not (partially) offset the lost EU students.'

The report estimates that '[t]he total loss to the UK economy could amount to almost £2 billion a year in steady state'. This includes '£928 million a year less from the detrimental impact on universities' supply chains (known as "the indirect and induced effects")'. That loss of £928 million a year from direct university supply chains only partially accounts for lost income for academic bookshops, challenged by both declining institutional and student income.

Last year nearly 135,000 EU students attended courses at UK Universities. According to a report by Anna Fazackerley, 'Universities UK, the vice-chancellors' umbrella body, is warning that without action universities will face "sudden, steep declines" in EU student numbers post-Brexit' (Fazackerley 2018). At the moment, EU students pay the same fees as UK students, but after Brexit will pay the same fees as any other international student: up to £20,000/course. While decision makers such as Professor Julia Black of LSE have claimed that regarding any fall in undergraduate student numbers, 'we are pretty confident we could make up the difference with strong UK students. But at graduate level we are more exposed in some areas if we lose European students completely. We would have to rethink what we teach and how.' Professor Black also sees a threat to staffing levels in some departments, where many lecturers are EU citizens. Nigel Carrington, vice-chancellor of the University of the Arts London, stated, 'EU students are among the highest performers at UAL. They deliver significant creative and financial benefits to the UK creative industries after graduation. If, as expected, EU student numbers drop by 60% in the UK following Brexit, the hit on university fee income will be the least of our worries.'

In consequence, Carrington states, 'Universities . . . are drawing up lists of courses that could face closure after Brexit and lobbying the government to save them by changing its policy on student fees.'

In some cases, the impending drop in EU student numbers specifically and student numbers as a whole has already impacted. The University of Manchester claimed plans to make 171 staff roles redundant were necessitated by issues including 'greater global competition, reductions in public funding, exchange rate fluctuations, a potential decline in student numbers and research income, new private providers, the new Teaching Excellence Framework, the uncertainties of Brexit and further increases in costs arising

from pensions and inflation' (Pidd 2017). At Heriot Watt, making 100 staff redundant, '[a] university statement cited a "Brexit effect"', which had 'creat[ed] uncertainty affecting postgraduate uptake', as well as 'the UK government's immigration policies and messaging'. Other negative factors included 'a shortfall in overseas fee-paying students due to a world-wide economic downturn' and 'a decline in the success rates' for European Union research grants' (Reisz 2017).

Anecdotally, academic bookshops across the UK have already seen a drop in the number of EU students and a rise in the number of non-EU students, particularly from China (Hawker 2018g). This observation is backed up by figures from the UK Council for International Student Affairs (UKCISA), which states of International (non UK) students in the 2016–17 academic year:

> The number of Chinese students far exceeds any other nationality; almost one third of non-EU students in the UK are from China. This is the only country showing a significant increase in student numbers (14% rise since 2012–13). (UK Council for International Student Affairs 2018)

There are also substantial numbers of students from Malaysia, from America, from India, and from Hong Kong, as well as many other countries – in total, including EU students, the number of non-UK students studying in the UK in 2016–17 was 442,375. Yet at the point of writing, Prime Minister Teresa May aims to include overseas students as a body within the Government's target of 100,000 immigrants a year or less, post Brexit (Waugh 2018). That inclusion would be financially disastrous for UK Universities – and for academic bookshops.

2 The Shop Front: the Value of Discount

Assuming that the academic bookshop has a student body to provide with books, it is the action of persuading those students or the institutions serving those students to purchase text which is the ultimate goal of that bookshop. Unless the majority of academic bookshops can make sufficient

profit to cover costs and/or offer enough of a return on capital to share-holders or stakeholders that their investment remains attractive, the book-shop becomes an unviable entity. 'Capital' here is defined as monetary or social, for there are academic bookshops providing social capital for stake-holders whose financial subsidies allow the bookshop to continue. The Leicester University Bookshop, for example, operated at a loss for several years until closure in 2016 (Campbell 2016b). Amazon, notoriously, oper-ated at a loss for nearly a decade and to this day prioritises reinvestment over shareholder returns. For the vast majority of academic bookshops, however, continued viability depends on continued financial profitability, and thus on profit margin.

The cost of selling text is subject to legislative pressure as well as market forces, and thus in discussing pricing it is necessary to evaluate the impact of both local and global taxation. Discounting is perceived to be an active choice by the bookseller, and the factors influencing both the decision to discount – or not – and the impact of those decisions are discussed at length. In particular, the evaluation of local markets – in the UK, the United States and Asia – serves to describe both global and local influencers, and book-seller responses to local financial ecology in a global marketplace.

Methods of attracting customers to academic bookshops are not solely financial, and options other than the discounting of books, and the market-ing of those discounts to customers, are discussed below. For most academic bookshop managers and staff, however, the engine of the shop's survival is the relationship between the cost of purchasing text and the percentage of profit gained in selling: the mechanisms of margin, discount, and profit before costs.

2.1 Impact of VAT Legislation

There are two major legislative actions which have impacted and continue to impact on academic booksellers and customers in the UK: the withdrawal of the net book agreement, and the application – or not – of VAT to book prices.

One of the most familiar phrases of the bookselling industry is 'the demise of the net book agreement', a loaded descriptor of an event which was at the time welcomed by bookselling chains and the Publishers

Association (Utton 2010). The NBA was a voluntary agreement between publishers and booksellers, dating from 1900, which allowed publishers to set a net price for books and booksellers to sell at that price and no other, with exceptions for certain named customers (libraries and books clubs, for example). In 1994, the Office of Fair Trading announced a review of the NBA, undertaken by the Restrictive Practices Court (RPC). After considerable consultation, in March 1997 the RPC stated that the NBA was no longer in the public interest, and it was declared illegal.

Value Added Tax (VAT), the UK sales tax, also impacts on pricing. Physical text is zero-rated, although any text which is accompanied by a CD, DVD or other non-printed resource material is liable for VAT on that non-printed accompaniment. However, 'the supply of text by electronic transmission (including e-books), via the Internet, or similar means is also standard-rated. Such supplies are of services, not of goods, and different VAT rules will apply to them' (HM Revenue and Customs 2016). Industry representatives across Europe have lobbied for the removal or standardisation of VAT on e-books. The situation is in flux. In March 2017, The ECJ (European Court of Justice) ruled that VAT on e-books cannot be reduced, because 'they formed part of a specific VAT regime [of] e-commerce, where clear and uniform rules needed to apply' (Campbell 2017). However, the European Commission has proposed 'to enable Member States to apply the same VAT rate to e-publications such as e-books and online newspapers as for their printed equivalents'. Member states have to agree to the specific e-book exemption proposal before it is implemented (Cowdrey 2016). Currently, as of spring 2019, region-specific VAT is still applicable to e-book sales: the rate of VAT charged is a function of government legislation and is thus subject to change, provided (in the EU) the country maintains a weighted average VAT rate of at least 12 per cent.

2.1.1 Pressure to Discount: NET Book Agreement and Internet Sales

Of these two legislative influences on text profit margins, it is the demise of the NBA which has had the most impact on academic bookshops. In 1996, this was not the issue it later became. Publisher Wiley predicted that discounting would not affect academic textbooks:

STM books are generally so specialised that price reductions will not stimulate enough extra sales to cover the profits lost from lower pricing. Likewise, college textbooks are already aggressively priced in order to attract the maximum number of individual purchasers.

A year before, Jeff Bezos had started selling books out of his garage in Seattle, Washington (Amazon.co.uk 2018b). Amazon.co.uk opened for trade in 1998. Amazon's deep discounting on media products, including academic text, appealed to online shoppers, and proved such a successful sales strategy that by 2009 the American Booksellers Association wrote to the Department of Justice claiming that Amazon was indulging in predatory pricing, forcing rivals out of business through loss-leading offers (Trachtenberg 2009). The company was also implicated in *United States* v. *Apple Inc.*, in which Apple was accused of colluding with the major book publishers to raise the price of e-books above Amazon's then preferred $9.99 price point (Cote 2014). In both cases, Amazon proved that it was in fact making a profit on both physical and digital book sales and therefore could not legally be accused of predatory pricing. In fact, Amazon adheres to a business model in which cash flow, leveraged through cross-selling, online services, and third party sales, rather than absolute profit, is the driver for success (Evans 2014). Thus, the low margins inherent in academic textbook supply, directly impacting on academic bookshops, are less impactful on Amazon and other 'big box' text suppliers with their far broader range of goods and services.

The Bookseller's Association, measuring market share, states that by 2005 online suppliers had achieved a significant 11 per cent market share of the total UK book market, up from 5 per cent in 2001, and inclusive of academic text (The Booksellers Association 2014). At the time, Kes Nielsen, senior vendor relations manager at Amazon, said, 'we took hold with students and academics, and they are still important as a share of the business' (Stewart 2005).

Although many publishers affirmed to booksellers that Amazon and other online suppliers received the same margin as academic bookshops, the majority of bookshops felt unable to match online discounts in store

(Hawker 2005–18). Nevertheless, as shoppers became increasingly accustomed to both shopping online and to the expectation of discount, academic bookshops felt considerable social and financial pressure to discount (Centre for Competition Policy 2008). (As discussed previously, Blackwell UK made the corporate decision to price match against online retailers in 2016.) Notably, and despite Wiley's comments, Alison Baverstock writes in 1990 that academic publishers were already building into title pricing models the capacity to discount (Baverstock 1990), although some academic publishers continue to this day pricing to cost rather than to market (Hawker 2016–18).

Before discussing discount models and their impact on bottom line, establishing a baseline profit margin provides a useful point of reference. This is easier said than done, however, for each bookshop makes its own negotiation with publishers over margin, and most bookshops consider that information commercially privileged. In addition, bookshops will negotiate extra discount for bulk sales, for promotions, for new titles and for local authors, and will also undertake base rate renegotiation on the basis of increased sales. They may also accept a lesser margin from a wholesaler as an acceptable cost for expedited delivery. Publishers will offer extra discounts or extended credit for bulk sales, for promoting a particular imprint or new title and for securing promotional space. In other words, margin is variable, and discussions of margin can only be estimates.

That said, bookseller Ron Johns of the closing independent Plymouth University Bookshop complained in 2016, 'we were finding it impossible to run a bookshop on 30% discount from publishers' (Campbell 2016f). However, books are not the only items bookshops sell, and many have branched into non-book product (cf. John Smith's) taking advantage of higher margins on stationery, apparel and gifts, often 50–60 per cent. A bookshop's overall margin, therefore, is likely to be higher than 30 per cent.

To put that 30 per cent margin in context, the average margin for clothing retail is 55–62 per cent (Claypoole 2018), for furniture, up to 900 per cent (Lazzari 2018). This margin is baseline profit, the markup on goods sold before any further costs are taken into account. Wages, rent, rates, utilities, insurance and all other retail expenditure must be taken out of baseline profit, gross profit, before a bookshop's financial success or failure can be assessed. In addition to these ongoing expenses, the bookseller must also maintain

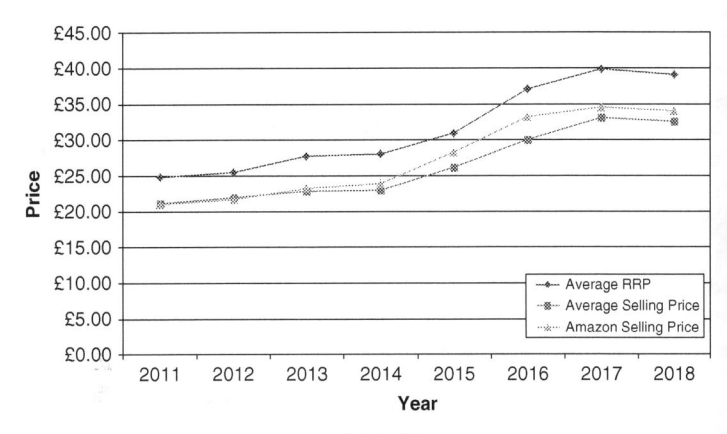

Figure 1. Textbook Discounting 2011–2018

Data drawn from records of discounted textbooks, Blackwell South Bridge, in the late August/early September of each year referenced. Base data has been manipulated to exclude custom books, custom packs and titles unavailable from Amazon at point of data collection.

working capital, or books sold cannot be replaced. Thus, every discount option below, removing 3–20 per cent from baseline margin, impacts the overall financial viability of the bookshop with greater severity than the same discounts in other areas of retail. Nevertheless, almost every academic bookshop follows at least one and usually many of the discount options described below, and an analysis of stickered, discounted sales (see Figure 1) shows an increasing interval between a book's RRP and its discounted price.

2.1.2 Discounting Options for the Academic Bookshop

Easy to manage, promote and understand, the value of a traditional discount on a single text depends only on the degree to which the store is willing to compromise publisher margin – or the level of additional margin a publisher will provide in order to finance that retail discount. For example, a bookseller selling 10 copies of a textbook at £56.99, with a margin of 33 per cent,

will make a profit of £188.07, but if that textbook is discounted by £5, the bookseller will make £138.47. In order to make the same amount of profit as an undiscounted text, the bookseller needs to sell 14 copies (£193.29). Should the publisher offer, or be persuaded to offer, an additional 5 per cent of margin to total 40 per cent, income after discount for the bookshop would rise to £17.80 for each book. An additional two copies of the book must be sold to maintain pre-discount profit levels. Yet without discounting, the bookshop may sell only one or two copies, rendering the pre- or post-discount financial analysis moot: with few or no sales, the bookshop is unviable.

2.1.2.1 Discounting options: multibuy discounts
Optional purchases, study skills books and general reference texts, are often higher-margin texts which can be discounted to purchasers as part of a multibuy offer – the familiar buy one, get one free; buy one, get one half price; or three-for-two options offered by high street bookshops as well as academic bookshops. Because of the complex price mechanism involved, no online retailer yet offers this variety of discounting. Generally multibuys require a considerable margin offer from the publisher, 55 per cent or more, with both publisher and bookshop hoping to make up in volume sales the losses from that higher margin: the bookshop's overall multibuy margin reduces to around 30 per cent.

2.1.2.2 Discounting options: pack discounts (academic books)
Academic book packs are an option increasingly popular with students, bookshops and publishers, particularly for text-heavy first- and second-year courses. Consulting with course leaders, the bookshop arranges a discounted bundle or pack of texts for students. For example, Blackwell South Bridge's current First Year First Semester Law Pack includes three textbooks for the three compulsory courses, plus a copy of statutes necessary for an open book exam. Extra margin from each of the four publishers involved funds the bundle price: the average margin is 39 per cent, the discount to the student is £24.98, and the margin for the bookshop after discount is about 24 per cent.

The reassurance to the student of having the 'right books' is priceless. In 2017, an informatics first-year student complained on the shop floor about the lack of a pack for their compulsory courses. This comment, passed on to

the lecturers concerned, resulted in a two-book pack for 2018 which achieved a 65 per cent sell-through rate.

2.1.2.3 Discounting options: price matching

While the options above are fixed-price discounts, amenable to online and in-store marketing, and easy to convey to students by way of a slide or presentation, price match offers are less easy to quantify. Price match offers, where a bookshop promises to match the lowest available legitimate text offer, are financed via intersecting provisions. For example, a publisher might offer a pot of money to a bookshop in order to fund nonspecific price offers, effectively replacing increased margin on a number of single texts; or a bookshop might obtain extra margin on specific titles but use that extra margin to fund price matching across all the publisher's titles. In either case, in store, the bookshop's assumption is that price matching will not be universal: full-priced margin on some sales will enable price-matched sales on others. For online retailers, however, price matching is attained via a complex series of algorithms that are necessarily dependent on a variable price point – automatically matching or undercutting Amazon's prices, for example, is a risky strategy, dependent on rigorous cost control for a seller.

2.1.2.4 Discounting options: dynamic pricing

Although dynamic pricing is often perceived to be a product of Internet-enabled pricing, in fact the discounts offered in store to privileged groups date back to the book groups and lending library memberships of the Enlightenment. Store membership card owners, book club members, Society of Author card holders, local educational institute employees, and any number of local discount holders have access to discounted text via their local bookshop and occasionally online, through promotional offers and permanent percentage discounts.

Electronic in-store dynamic pricing is seldom seen in the UK but is utilised in bricks-and-mortar stores where there is a direct, immediate relationship between online and in-store pricing. For example, Amazon's physical bookstores offer a Prime discount to Prime members and a higher price for the same text to non-Prime members. Chinese bookstores, with automatic checkout desks, offer dynamic pricing via purchase app.

However the pricing is applied, the bookshop's expectation is that dynamic pricing is financed via increased volume sales.

2.1.2.5 Discounting options: bulk discounts to institutions

For many academic bookshops, and increasingly for online retailers, discounted sales to institutional purchasers are vital to continued viability. Institutional discounting can be local or national, and relate to a single purchasing body or a UK-wide purchase framework: the Southern Universities Purchasing Consortium, for example, covers ninety institutions, and offers a two-year purchasing agreement worth in excess of £90m/year, awarded to thirteen suppliers (SUPC 2017). Although participating institutions can order 'off framework', the savings offered by approved suppliers, and the ease of ordering through integrated purchase systems, ensure that for aligned institutions the vast majority of orders will be placed with approved suppliers. For smaller academic bookshops, therefore, tendering for approval on a purchase framework used by their local educational institution can be vital to continued cash flow.

2.1.3 Sustainability, Sales, and Margin

However a bookseller discounts, the underlying mechanism that the discounting bookseller must establish – whether this is the algorithms of an online retailer or the swift decision making of a single bookseller with a table of books and a customer asking for a price-match – is that discounting will attract enough additional purchasers to balance lost profit with increased sales. Thus, advertising. There is no point in providing a discount if students, institutions or favoured purchasers do not know that the discount exists: how else does a bookseller attain the extra sales required for sustainability?

Equally, the influence of publisher margin can also be seen. The more margin a publisher offers a bookshop, the more margin that bookshop can invest in discount. The lever of persuasion has to be enhanced sales, in order to persuade a publisher to offer that extra margin, to persuade students to buy from the bookshop rather than elsewhere and to make that extra profit needed to finance the deal for both publisher and bookseller.

Thus an academic bookshop, online or off, with a targeted discount plan – knowledge of lecturer and course, student numbers and purchase patterns – has an excellent lever to persuade publishers to work with the bookshop. While some publishers will require this information before offering extra margin on any particular title, a bookshop which offers knowledgeable leverage unprompted is likely to see considerably more success than a bookshop which is uninformed and ill-prepared. Bookshops do not deserve extra margin from publishers merely by virtue of being a bookshop; but a viable plan to make additional sales, especially on an ongoing basis, does justify that extra financial support and works for both parties.

No matter how hard a bookshop works on negotiation with publishers and marketing to students, there is no doubt that discounting impacts on a bookshop's financial viability. Bookshops as a whole work on breath-takingly low margins, as discussed, when compared to the retail industry as a whole, and academic bookshops work on even lower gross margins than general bookshops: Michael Kaplan, of the successful independent Miami chain Books & Books, suggests 40 per cent (Sandler 2013), Wainwright, in the UK, 35 per cent (Wainwright 2005). Academic margins are 5–10 per cent lower; and of course, this is gross profit margin, before establishment, staffing and overhead costs are considered. It is no wonder that the UK bookselling industry has seen a succession of closures, such as Leicester in 2016, Plymouth in 2016, Portsmouth in 2018, and Queen's University Bookshop in 2011 (Onwuemezi 2018b). Queen's University Manager Tim Smith cited looming unprofitability: 'we have always been above the line but next year we will fall below the line. I don't know how we (independent booksellers) can do it anymore. Certainly the academic model has reached a tipping point now, it is unsustainable' (Campbell 2011). Even general bookshop Waterstone's, returning to profitability after years of loss-making trading, cited 'cost savings and a shift away from selling low margin academic course books into more profitable products like stationery and toys' (Wood 2018).

So, why discount? Successful independent bookshop owner Robert Topping, notoriously, does not discount his books. 'If you believe enough, you can make a book sell,' he says. 'I have to pay the bills myself, so I can

see if it works' (Beckett 2009). For years after the rise of the online book retailers, academic publishers like Wiley and Taylor and Francis argued that students would buy textbooks without discount. Pearson still insists that students should and will pay the full cost of a title, arguing that the quality of text contained in the title is worth the purchase price, although this does not stop the publisher offering discounts online themselves for direct purchase (Hawker 2018f). Student focus groups, however, do not concur.

2.1.4 Student Demand

A 2018 survey funded by the new Office for Students set out to define 'value for money' – student experience, or outcome? 'Do students feel they are receiving value for money? Do student perceptions of value for money evolve as they go from school to higher education, and then into the world of work? What can higher education providers – and the OfS – do to help improve the value students perceive they are getting from the considerable investment they have made in higher education?' (Leishman 2018). The study covered tuition fees and other fees and costs incurred during student studies, surveying 6,000 current students, recent graduates and school leavers in England and Scotland (Office for Students 2018c). Of these students, 24 per cent felt that they were not fully informed about costs of study, with the main factors cited being costs of accommodation, books and paying for extracurricular activities.

> 'The price for books that you "have to have" but only look
> at once is disgusting.'
> 'I find the cost of resources fair. It definitely helps that the
> university invests in additional resources to help reduce the
> cost to students, e.g. textbooks and online textbooks.'
> 'I was not told . . . [h]ow expensive books would be that
> are compulsory for the course we have to pay on our own.'
> (Office for Students 2018c).

Eighty-five per cent felt that tuition fees should be used to pay for library resources: 58 per cent felt that the institution should provide essential course books, although only 81 per cent felt that the quality of library facilities

should be a 'very important' factor in demonstrating institution value for money. Ninety-eight per cent, however, felt that library facilities were either very or somewhat important. For academic bookshops in particular, it is useful to see what information students would prefer to see in terms of investigating value for money:

> The most popular option was seeing a breakdown of how the provider spends its fee income (88%). 86% would like to see top-up information on the income and expenditure at their provider, while 83% of our respondents would find it helpful to compare the costs incurred by their course compared to other courses at other universities. (Office for Students 2018a).

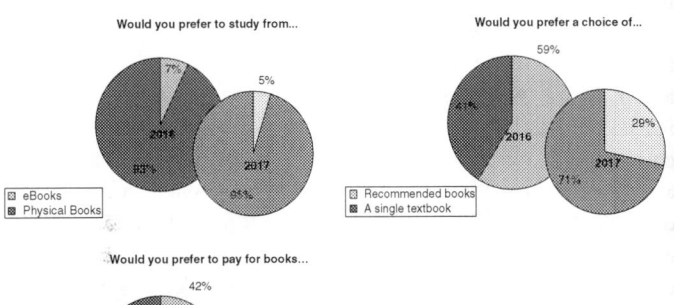

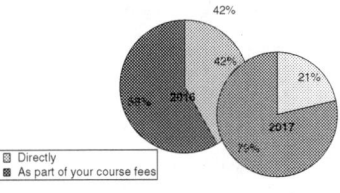

Figure 2. Student Survey 2016, 2017

Data drawn from yearly student survey, Blackwell South Bridge, Edinburgh, September–October 2016 and 2017. Leaflets with survey questions (see Figure 4) were handed out to students at the till point and on campus. Participants were entered into a prize draw.

A similar range of conclusions are reflected in student surveys at Blackwell Edinburgh, where, in 2016, 45 per cent of 748 students questioned felt that course books should be provided by their institution – although 55 per cent felt that they preferred to choose whether to buy, rent or loan their textbooks using their own funds. In 2017, that percentage had shifted to 50 per cent apiece. Every student contacted by Green Leaf's 2017 survey of Resource Provision in Higher Education thought that 'the university should include the cost of resources in the fees' but were prepared to pay for some resources, although the most any of them had spent was £100 over two years (Bennett *et al.* 2017). It is worth noting that none of the Green Leaf students surveyed attended institutions with campus bookshops; the Edinburgh students did have access to an academic bookshop. These same views were common to students of the annual Academic, Professional and Specialist Group booksellers' student focus groups, surveyed at conferences from 2013 to 2017.

Several useful conclusions can be drawn from this research for the academic bookseller. Firstly, and most importantly, students do consider access to excellent learning resources to be of importance in their studies. Secondly, textbook costs rank highly in an index of student perceptions of expenditure. Obviously, the concept of 'no-fees-added' courses as a student attractor is an argument that academic bookshops can take to campus leaders, pushing for institutional purchase of text, digital or physical, along with student retention and TEF metrics accreditation; but also of consideration is the value students ascribe to openness concerning the use of course fees and the identification of additional costs. For academic bookshops providing text for individual student purchase, this is a perfect argument for preregistration marketing, first lecture presentations, and VLE compatible slides, listing course books, physical and digital availability, and cost. Moreover, in terms of that cost, students are clearly concerned by their expenditure and thus attuned to perceptions of value. At Blackwell Edinburgh, for example, medical students have been asked to buy the same five textbooks since 2007. On-campus sales year to year have been tracked against online discounts and pirated download availability. Student numbers and degree of recommendation have remained the same: download availability remained constant. The influencing factor for sales was the

online discounted price, even when students were in the shop (Hawker 2013).

2.1.5 International Impacts

Legislative market impact, pressure to discount, and institutional purchase are not influencers unique to the UK. The same is true for academic bookshops across the world. Models of response, however, do differ, and it is worth taking a brief look and considering if any options are currently relevant to the UK market.

2.1.5.1 United States

Although UK and US markets share many of the same publishers and titles, the most impactful US influence on the UK lies in perception of the UK textbook market as reprehensively over-priced (University of Stanford 2016). A 2016 post, '£630 per student: the cost of paper textbooks' for example, draws on US textbook pricing rather than UK pricing (University of Essex 2016) – while in the year of the Kirstaeng decision, UK titles were on average 82.5 per cent cheaper in the UK (Hawker 2016e). But many of the arguments for and initiatives taking root in the UK market, open access textbooks (if not journal and monograph publication), faculty, library and new university press editions, and the move to VLE-based online learning, often utilising deconstructed text or faculty-generated text, originate from the United States and its higher-priced marketplace.

James V. Koch describes the US market as, historically, a trust economy, 'in which students buy textbooks because their trusted faculty members tell them to do so.' However, the market has become dominated by five publishers, Cengage, Pearson, McGraw-Hill, Worth and Wiley, who 'now appear to control more than 90% of the *new* textbook market.' Bundling with additional resources and/or online learning platforms, planned obsolescence with frequent new editions, importation bans, and custom editions serve to bind students into that lucrative recommended text market. The average price of a textbook in 2012 was $183.29, an 812 per cent increase on 1978, a period over which the US consumer price index rose by 250 per cent (Koch 2014). These price increases have become a notorious charge on students already burdened by tuition fees, and this has had severe

consequences for the US textbook market. Students are choosing to circumvent new text sales to access physical text.

The Book Industry Study Group suggests that approximately two-thirds of all textbook units used by students now are purchased used, rented, borrowed, shared, or copied. Their report found that 25% of students in 2012 photocopied orscanned some textbooks and 19% acquired their book from a pirate website (Mitchell 2014).

Student Monitor's just-released survey of 1,200 students revealed that the average full-time undergraduate student downloaded 1.2 textbooks per semester from possibly illegal file-sharing sites (Koch 2014). The survey suggests that 40 per cent plus of all student textbook purchases now are used books, and that e-books now account for about 8 per cent. However, 'this latter rapidly than other segments.'

To put these concerns in context, The College Board estimates a year's textbook costs for a full-time US student as $1,250 (College Board 2018), while the National Association of College Stores estimates that the average student actually spent $579 (admittedly 2016–17) on all course materials, including stationery and printing, over the course of a year (National Association of College Stores 2017).

In terms of assistance with textbook costs, many US students can apply for grants and financial aid from their institution, their state, or private foundations, some of which are explicitly for textbook acquisition (College Scholarships 2017). Assistance via sales tax exemptions in the United States is variable, applied on a state-by-state basis.

It was the high prices of textbooks in the United States which led, in 2008, to student Supap Kirtsaeng asking friends to send books from Thailand, where prices were far lower. He then resold texts to fellow students. John Wiley & Co took legal action. In 2013 the case reached the Supreme Court, which ruled that 'first-sale doctrine applies to all lawful copyrighted works, including those made abroad'. This decision effectively required global price parity for identical textbooks printed and sold in the United States and elsewhere. Although there was a brief expectation the decision would lead to lower US textbook prices, this was not the case, and instead publishers adopted US price parity worldwide, and then either produced cheaper region-restricted editions (Pearson's 'Global

International Editions', for example), altered their margin to booksellers to reflect both US price parity and region-specific deep discounting (John Wiley) or applied for Library of Congress exemptions for specific recommended textbooks sold abroad (Cengage). For some years, this created favourable conditions for UK booksellers, as the RRP shown on online websites reflected the US price, as required, while UK booksellers were selling at considerably below RRP. The effect is fading as new editions are produced and priced for the UK market.

For academic booksellers, the most impactful recent US initiative is likely to be the $5 million recently allocated by the FY18 omnibus appropriation bill to an 'Open Textbooks Pilot' programme in Fiscal Year 2018, awarded as competitive grants to institutions of higher education through the US Department of Education, giving 'special consideration to projects at institutions of higher education that demonstrate the greatest potential to achieve the highest level of savings for students through sustainable, expanded use of open textbooks in postsecondary courses offered by the eligible entity and expand the use of open textbooks'. The bill was introduced on March 21, 2018 and signed into law two days later (United States Government 2018).

2.1.5.2 Asian Markets

State-owned bookseller Xinhua, now dispersed into regionally controlled smaller chains, currently dominates the school textbook market across China (Liu 2018). Although by law school textbooks can only be sold at a minimal margin to private buyers and are supplied free to rural students (Pan 2016), legacy contracts allow Xinhua to dominate domestic textbook sales. Academic bookshops selling *xueshu shu*, or 'books in the fields of the social sciences and humanities, especially philosophy, history, political science, sociology, law', are also popular across China, having served to regularise the bookselling industry in the 1990s after the explosion of private bookshops in the late 1970s. Internet bookselling was adopted early in China and still contains vicious price wars between dominant companies Dangdang.com and JD.com, although marketplace sites such as Tmell.com (owned by corporate giant Alibaba) allow publishers to sell directly to the public, aiding profit margins. Chinese books are not subject to VAT,

although this exceptional privilege has only been accorded to private booksellers since 2013.

University textbooks are, in the main, English translations, imported and printed for the Chinese market or pirated editions, although the Chinese government is cautious about both source and content – banning, for example, textbooks printed in Taiwan or works considered to be ideologically unsound (Buckley 2015). The intense price pressure of the Chinese market has proved difficult for western text providers: Amazon.com, for example, has a small and falling market share. Controversies over content control (Cambridge University Press 2017), and the kidnapping of Hong Kong booksellers (Cowdrey 2018), also influence publishers and booksellers. The market is seen, however, as of growing importance to UK publishers, but also impacts on both UK academic booksellers and publishers as a major source of pirated digital and physical text (United States International Trade Commission 2010).

In other markets, academic publishers have pursued differing models, with some success. In the growing Indian market, for example, international publishers print locally and cheaply, pricing to the market: BookMap (Wischenbart 2018) suggests that the 2015 book market in India is worth $3.6 billion, roughly comparable to France in value, although the number of volumes sold is far greater. Publishers such as Cambridge University Press, Oxford University Press and Sage have established India-based publishing houses with flourishing region-specific outputs. Pearson, for example, markets Paul Deitel's *Java How to Programme* (10th edition) priced at RS899 ($13.22 or £9.84 as of May 2018) for the Indian market (Pearson Publishing Ltd 2018a). The same content was priced at $174.93 (£129.86, RS11,892.62) for the US market (Pearson Publishing Ltd 2018b). Inevitably, there is some import overlap, with one University of Edinburgh lecturer commenting of Riley's *Mathematical Methods for Physics and Engineering* that, 'Last year students purchased a very cheap edition. Could you import for us?' (Hawker 2017c). The edition turned out to be Indian, sold through the Amazon marketplace: the bookshop could not legally import. Similar local pricing and printing options are practiced in other markets with an established printer infrastructure such as Hong Kong and Macau, licensed and unlicensed: Oxford University Press is currently

Figure 3. Academic Bookshop, Beijing 北京

Modern academic Bookshop in Beijing, China. Photographs © Stephen Harwood, used by permission.

pursuing a prosecution against a printer in Belfast who is alleged to have openly advertised print on demand (POD) services with an itemised catalogue of university textbooks (Hawker 2018d).

2.1.6 Traditional and New Publishers on the Future of Text Pricing

Given the influences on pricing visible from the academic bookshop – the perception of overpricing, the pressure to discount, the student-led move towards lower priced second-hand, rented, open access or pirated text – what is remarkable about the textbook market is the choice made by the majority of academic publishers to prioritise high-value sales rather than bulk low-value sales. This was particularly apparent during the years 2008–2016, when larger UK/US publishers pursued an aggressive policy

of prioritising investment in digital development and direct institutional sales above individual sales through bookshops, combined with a policy of raising textbook prices in order to combat falling sales. The consequences for academic bookshops required careful management, particularly from 2012, when it became apparent that considerable publisher investment in purchasing educational software companies and consequent in-house digital development were not producing the expected shareholder returns, and publishing houses began to cut costs elsewhere.

Externally, academic bookshops found themselves facing an aggressive campaign by academic publishers to obtain direct institutional sales. While this proved a successful strategy in some areas, particularly in terms of journal sales to libraries, it has also led to a perception of academic publishers as inflexible and greedy. Adam Smith, interviewing Elsevier's director of access and policy Alicia Wise in 2014, among other complaints drew attention to the 15,000 academics who in 2012 boycotted Elsevier due to their business practices (Smith 2014). 'Business, it seems, has not been affected,' stated Smith dryly, mentioning Elsevier's recent stock value upgrade and move towards APC-funded publication. In some cases, publishers were prepared to circumvent or ignore existing local frameworks for institutional supply. 'We'll sort that out later,' said Kortext's Kevin Watt, with reference to the Scotland Excel purchase framework (Hawker 2018e). In others, the supply of textbooks proved an initial benefit to the publisher, but actually impacted profits in later years. 'It is short-sighted,' said Glenn Thomas, then of Pearson, pointing out that the initial enrolment fee for online textual provision was substantially more than the profit from a year's sales of physical books for the same course, but yearly renewal costs considerably less, and subsequent profits to the publisher are consequently reduced (Hawker 2016d).

With substantial investment of both capital and ideology in learning technology, academic publishers were also heavily investing in testing (Kane 2016), in credentialing (Belshaw 2016) and in the creation of platform-based inclusive education software (Cengage 2017). 'Publishers should move from translating print textbooks into digital form to creating truly digital courses that take advantage of everything the medium has to offer. Rather than thinking in terms of e-textbooks, publishers need to

develop "whole-course solutions" that deliver an entire class or instructional unit,' stated Allison Bailey in the 2014 consultancy report *The Digital Disruption of Education Publishing* (Bailey *et al.* 2014). Some publishers have gone further, moving into providing not only accredited online courses but establishing their own classroom-based schools and colleges (Kamenetz 2016). However, in a crowded marketplace, traditional publishers have repeatedly lost ground to native digital innovators. In 2013, Cengage filed for bankruptcy in order to restructure a \$5.8bn debt load (Edgecliffe-Johnson *et al.* 2013), while Pearson has issued five profit warnings since 2012, 'culminating in its biggest ever loss in 2016 of £2.5bn while shares slumped to a seven-year low' (Cowdrey 2017b). Publishers have been criticised for exploiting low-income students with for-profit schooling, and repeated system failure (Strauss 2016).

As a result of this change in focus, academic booksellers have not only confronted the immediate financial consequences of student sales lost to institutional publisher purchase, but the functional consequences of financial retrenchment and sharp price rises. It is not the publisher but the customer-facing bookseller who faces student and institutional rage over the increased price of new textbooks (Williams 2015). In addition, during 2012–2016, publisher redundancies at Cengage, McGraw-Hill and Pearson, and the consolidation of representation and Elsevier and other smaller publishers, left bookshops either without academic representatives or with remote contacts that had never seen the shop or institution they were servicing. New title awareness, textbook ordering, promotions and returns were all affected, along with systems failures in terms of delivery, invoicing and customer service provision, leading to a continuing breakdown of trust between bookshop and publishers.

Many academic bookshops, however, took advantage of this publisher absence to reposition themselves within their institutions. Booksellers, already the public face of book supply to students, took on many of the traditional functions of an active academic publisher, recommending textbooks, becoming involved in course design, serving as a conduit for review and desk copies of textbooks, consulting on textbook publication and referring academics to publishers, and proposing and supporting study skills and careers events. Committed to supplying text, but free from the

single-source commercial imperative of a traditional publisher's representative, and in addition locally based on or near campus, the academic bookseller had the capacity to become a trusted partner to course leaders and innovators within their academic community. One fundamental area in which the bookseller has traditionally had little influence, but now had tools to manage, was the issue of textbook price, often the fundamental image of the campus bookshop in a customer's eyes.

There is a certain irony in the ideological commitment of publishers to digital technology, while students stubbornly continued to purchase physical text. This became apparent to publishers from 2016 onwards, leading to a resurgence of publisher interest in promoting traditional textbook sales through bookshops (Campbell 2016e) and the consequent reappointment of academic representatives (Campbell 2018). However, both the perception of textbook prices and the real textbook price increases over the previous few years, the withdrawal of campus presence and an increasing ideological opposition to corporatisation left some publishers with a credibility gap on traditional campuses. Academic booksellers are in a position to be able to exploit this situation, able to argue for extra discount for students as a necessity rather than a luxury if sales are to be maintained, with additional financial incentive required for sales growth. With the feedback cycle of student to academic and institution now involving resource provision, textbook price as well as suitability has become an issue for course leaders, a situation which a local bookseller can leverage in publisher negotiations. Honesty and transparency has also proved to be useful leverage, both in terms of student and academic awareness of pricing strategy and in terms of publisher trust that the bookshop will hold to any pricing agreement. For many shop-floor academic booksellers, the provision of the best price possible to students impacted by both student debt and the increasing cost of living has become a point of pride. For the bookshop manager, the increased sales from discounted text have become the means by which the bookshop survives as a financially viable institution.

For publishers, however, pricing strategy varies. For the larger university presses, Oxford University Press and Cambridge University Press, both registered charities, the production pricing strategy for both trade and academic text includes the capacity to discount, while UK RRP for

individual textbooks tends to be lower than that of commercial publishers. For publishers whose interest has been largely in digital development – Cengage, Pearson, McGraw-Hill and to a lesser extent Wiley – UK RRPs have risen above the cost of inflation. Wiley has been willing to compensate with an aggressive discounting programme. Cengage and McGraw-Hill have discounted to students once benefits have been demonstrated, while Pearson has been notoriously unwilling to discount at all to any institution, bookshop or student. Pearson's Simon Pollard stated in 2017 that students should be willing to pay a premium price for premium content, unwilling to recognise that bookshop and Internet retailing discounts to those students have helped Pearson retain their share of the physical textbook market – while Pearson UK discounts on their own web store for direct sales. Smaller academic publishers have also accepted discounting as a retail strategy, with Taylor and Francis, Sage and Lippincourt all building the capacity to discount into their sales strategy. For the majority of smaller academic publishers, a cogent argument backed up by sales figures will generally prove a bookshop's point when looking for student discounts. For example, publisher discounts combined with bookshop contributions at Blackwell South Bridge have meant that the average discount to students over the past seven years has been 16.15 per cent of retail price. (Kirstaeng titles, with their 80 per cent–plus discounts, have been removed from this calculation.) Gross and net takings, and quantity of books sold, have risen in every year from 2011 to 2017: anecdotal evidence suggests that the bookshop has embedded itself within student tradition not only as the cheapest supplier, but as a trusted supplier.

Given this situation, where there is an unsurprisingly positive correlation between the discounted text and sales volume, together with a continuing interest in physical text, the interests and strategy of bookshops and publishers are surprisingly divergent. The logical conclusion, on this evidence, would suggest that the 'pile it high, sell it cheap' sales strategy of, for example, retailers like Lidl or Aldi, might work equally well for textbooks in the UK, and this is in effect the sales strategy of Internet retailers. Publishers, on the other hand, seeking to maintain a premium product, are committed to premium pricing, albeit with (generally speaking) the capacity to discount built in to that price. Yet given the decreasing costs of POD production, the

increasing flexibility of digital printing, and the continuing demand for physical books, it is remarkable that publishers have not adopted a similar sales strategy for UK and US markets as for their Asian markets – to continue the supermarket analogy, a 'value range' of textbooks with low production values, complimented by a 'premium' range with additional features (colour printing and/or access to digital resources, for example). In a marketplace where value has become the ultimate sales driver, this would seem a logical step.

To many publishers and bookshops, such a 'race to the bottom' would appear anathema. The core purpose of both publisher and bookshop is after all, no matter how a mission statement or corporate motto is phrased, to make money. 'The only thing we can't fight,' said then Academic, Professional and Specialist Booksellers Group chairman Gareth Hardy in 2015, discussing piracy and open access text, 'is a free book.' It is to this end that the entire structure of textbook discounting, margin management and marketing outreach has been developed across the Internet and in store by academic booksellers, directed at students, academics and institutions. And yet experience shows that in fact, free books may be exactly what the market needs.

3 Remerchandising Academic Text

The shifting ecology of academic publishing and bookselling may have left some publishers and bookshops struggling, but for others it has been an invigorating and enabling force. As well as the development of digital text and analytics, there has been a renewed academic interest in production and distribution of all academic text, seen in the UK rise of the New University Presses (Adema 2016) and of academic-led presses (Radical Open Access Collective 2016), the Academic Book of the Future project, the JISC-sponsored *institution as e-book publisher* project (JISC 2015) and Research England's REF2021 move towards requiring open access monograph publication (Hill 2018a) – and indeed in the *Gatherings* monograph series. Distribution innovation can be seen in the rise of open access textbooks (Open Access Textbooks Project 2018) and associated business models (Open Access Directory 2018), and in the 'shop indie' movement embracing

independent academic bookshops. For bookshops working with local academics, students and publishers, new forms of academic text mean new collaborators, customers and routes to market.

3.1 Digital Text

For larger academic publishers, digitising text very quickly became part of their production process, enabled by the move to digital printing and by the earlier transition of journal publication to digital forms. The first mechanised text was produced in 1949 by Ángela Ruiz Robles (Ruiz 2017), the first digital document created in 1971 (Hart 2017) and by 1993 early adopters were publishing e-books as a matter of course. Self-publishing was also established early on, with writers using .rtf and .html formatting and programmers creating the Open eBook format, which would lead to the industry standard .epub. Early commercial e-book publishers tended to use Adobe .pdf files, effectively an image of the physical textbook's content page by page. Early commercial e-books also lacked DRM (Digital Rights Management) coding and were swiftly pirated: by 2008, Blackwell South Bridge could source pirated editions of almost all major textbooks.

By 2009, when Amazon's propriety e-reader Kindle launched in the UK (BBC 2009), sparking the 'digital revolution' for general readers and publishers, academic e-books had already developed to include enhanced content. Medical book publishers were swift innovators in including video and interactive graphics (Elsevier 2018), while business and science course leaders and students quickly benefitted from enhanced text featuring quizzes, lecture notes and slides (Pearson Publishing Ltd 2018c). From a publisher's point of view, these options added additional value to textbooks for students, and were selling points to lecturers. And with students forced to purchase one-off access codes, the second-hand market for physical text and the pirate economy for digital text were both curtailed. Therefore, although the 'digital revolution' had a considerable impact on academic readers looking for straightforward text and on academic publishers who were only interested in straightforward digitisation, student-focused textbook publication had already, deliberately, moved past the technical capacity of most e-readers and platforms.

Digital text was available to students in a number of options. Direct digital purchase through the publisher's website or platform was the preferred option for many digital innovators, but for many academic bookshops the digital/physical pack was and remains the standard model for students. Access to digital resources was provided via CD-ROM, individual access codes or URLs supplied with the physical text; later development involved lecturers dispatching access codes following confirmed purchase, either via the student or via the institution.

Apart from the capacity to stock and sell digital text themselves, available to some but not all booksellers, the consequences for the academic bookshop were considerable. With many institutions reluctant at that point to move towards direct purchase, but supportive of enhanced material, booksellers benefitted from students needing to purchase new copies of textbooks with access to digital material. For booksellers working with lecturers, honest conversations around access, second-hand provision and enhanced or non-enhanced versions of text aided the positioning of the bookshop within the decision-making process. In addition, the early digitisation of textbooks meant that academic bookshops were already accustomed to absorbing some loss of income to pirated text and had noticed that possession of digital text did not eliminate student desire for physical text. Many UK students were both torrenting digital text and purchasing physical text, an observation that would enable later bookshop involvement in open access textbooks.

Although for many digital natives, and for publishers moving into the digital market, the future of text was digital alone, the debate over physical and digital text continues. There is considerable research suggesting that outcomes for students are improved with the use of digital text and learning strategies: '94% of students say that digital learning technology helps them retain new concepts' and '60% think that digital learning technology has improved their grades' (McGraw-Hill Education 2017b). For digital text users 'e-textbooks can prove to be extremely popular and widely used, mainly for obtaining snippets of information and for fact finding. Although the main reason cited for using e-books was ease of access and convenience' (Nicholas *et al.* 2014), research indicates that 'there is some evidence that reading on the screen produces lower levels of comprehension and retention

compared with reading on the page, at least among the current generation of university students' (Baron 2015). A 2016 study for JISC, covering 127 UK universities with questionnaire data from over 5,000 students, also found that 'generally, the e-book user was easily distracted and confused by the myriad navigational routes and display options, and the ability to move out of the e-book environment with ease and at will'. A smaller study by David Daniel and Krisztina Jakobsen (Daniel *et al.* 2018) tracked text scanning via eye movement, interviewed students and analysed learning comprehension. It found that while learning is possible from both formats, learning from e-textbooks takes longer and requires more effort to reach the same level of understanding, even in a controlled lab environment. 'Publishers can't change the way people read online,' Daniel said, 'but they can find new ways to format e-textbooks to make them more effective for how students learn best and prefer to interact with the product. We believe that science can help guide this process toward the development of more effective learning tools for all students.' Lauren M. Singer and Patricia A. Alexander found that while the majority of students learn more effectively from physical text, they perceive themselves as learning more effectively from digital text. 'Students judged their comprehension as better online than in print. Paradoxically, overall comprehension was better for print versus digital reading. The medium didn't matter for general questions (like understanding the main idea of the text). But when it came to specific questions, comprehension was significantly better when participants read printed texts' (Singer *et al.* 2017).

The continuing effectiveness of physical text as a route to comprehension has not gone unnoticed by students. A 2012 survey of 1,500 business and management students at the Ted Rogers School of Management, Ryerson University, found that 'the fluid and dynamic nature of digital content compared to the more consistent and predictable nature of information on paper appears to be a barrier to the acquisition of knowledge for the purpose of assessment. Students perceive paper textbooks as the best format for extended reading and studying and for locating information,' and recommended that 'for the moment, a choice of paper and e-textbooks should be offered to reflect the diverse learning styles.' Instructors, the authors suggest, should ensure a choice of formats is offered, and make sure

printing is enabled from any course available via a digital platform (McNeish 2012). A 2015 JISC-funded survey of 6,679 UK academics, repeating a similar 2012 survey, also found that 'academics' preference for using scholarly monographs in various ways in print format rather than digital format has only increased since the previous cycle of the survey; we have not observed a trend towards a format transition for monographs' (Wolff-Eisenberg *et al.* 2015).

However, for some readers, digital text has enabled their access to learning resources. Either built into a digital platform or available as add-ons, the ability to access text-to-speech editors and manipulate the appearance of text on screen is a vital resource for students for whom the physical book is physically or cognitively difficult to use. Accessibility through digital text is not just an ethical option: reasonable accommodation for students is a legal requirement (Equality Challenge Unit 2010).

For a bricks-and-mortar–based academic bookshop invested in physical text, both the scholarly assessment of physical text as a learning enabler and continuing student preference for physical text as well as or instead of digital text is a heartening conclusion, although conveying that preference to institutional decision makers remains vital. However, the advantages of digital text and of the analytics provided by digital learning platforms should not be underestimated: for both physical and digital text providers, the solution would appear to lie in enabling customer choice. In this marketplace, Kortext's partnerships with John Smith's and Blackwell bookshops would appear to be a sensible option for all partners and one worth pursuing for smaller campus bookshops.

3.2 Custom Books

Custom books, created specifically for a particular course, might or might not be digitised and might or might not contain access to enhanced material, but are required reading for a particular course. Institutional purchase guarantees a 100 per cent provision to students, but even where personal choice is involved, purchase rates may extend to 98 per cent of enrolled students (Hawker 2008–18). While some custom books are re-jacketed editions of existing textbooks and others chapter collections, also available as full works, some are the original work of a course lecturer, who therefore

has an emotional as well as professional investment in the text. For publishers, custom text has proved a remarkable success: in 2017, McGraw-Hill estimated that 29 per cent of its US textbook sales were custom books (McGraw-Hill Education 2017a), and for many academic bookshops their bestsellers are custom books.

For a bookseller, delivering a custom text tied to course, lecturer and student carries a moral responsibility to ensure that text is available when needed, and in a format suitable for the student. Publisher Pearson, with a brutal 'just-in-time' publishing schedule, has a notable history of failure to deliver despite timely ordering, but it is the bookshop which is faced with the understandable anger of lecturer and student. In these circumstances mitigation strategies can involve the issuing of full or first-chapter digital text; involving the course leader in negotiation at an early stage is recommended. Failure to deliver choice can also handicap students: the first year's supply of a successful Springer custom text for Edinburgh was only available digitally, but feedback from students forced course leader and publisher to provide additional physical copies. Alternatively, a similar Wiley custom text for a largely part-time blended learning master's degree at Napier University was initially available as both digital and physical copy, but lack of demand for the physical text meant that subsequent editions were available only as digital text.

Custom text is not confined to larger publishers. For example, Heriot Watt University has a thriving custom text publication programme, the Global Management Series (GMS) produced by Goodfellow Publishers, configured to provide for on-campus students in Scotland, Malaysia and Dubai, distance learners and students at the University's Associated Learning Partners completing syndicated courses. With the requirement that all students have equitable access to learning material, physical and digital text or both, through personal purchase, library provision, or VLE-linked digital text, publisher Goodfellows and campus bookseller Blackwell work together to supply individual and institutional purchase. Digital text is available online from both sources and through all campus libraries. Physical books are supplied as POD titles via industry supplier Marston Books, and although with a four-week turnaround for printing careful planning is essential to ensure student access, the price to all students

using these titles is favourably comparable to custom text from larger publishers.

Before commissioning the externally published GMS series, Heriot Watt University had a history of internal course-specific physical publications, notably for STEM and business-orientated students, printed internally and distributed via bookshop or school. Internal publication is a common continental model, generally less popular at UK universities, although the development of POD technology and the rise of both open access text and renewed interest in the university as publisher may well increase interest (for example, the *Institution as E-Textbook Publisher* project; JISC 2015). However, unless the institution is prepared to collaborate with digital learner vendors such as Kortext, devote considerable development time to their own hosting facilities and/or utilise relevant existing material, digital text will lack the additional resources or platform-based analytics which have proved valuable selling points for students and institutions using digital text for study.

3.3 Digital Platforms

For publishers, digital enhancement and custom text led to the development of digital platforms, which allowed both consolidation of digital resources and financial gatekeeping. Specific examples include the Mastering and MyLab resources for Pearson, or WebAssign from Cengage. Although platforms are set up for both personal and institutional access, the ideal for a publisher is to sell institutional access for each student, with or without physical text. The price tag, however, can be high – £26,000 for a year's access was quoted to one lecturer with 450 students in 2017 (Hawker 2017d), and with content carefully governed by the publisher the platform may not be ideal. It is impossible, for example, to upload additional material to most publisher platforms. This is not true, of course, of platform suppliers Kortext or VitalSource – Kortext in particular markets itself as a supplier of analytics rather than text – for both are multi-publisher sites, and Kortext has been known to host custom text as well as commercially available text. However, neither platform as yet can host the enhanced material common to academic textbooks and used as leverage in adoption strategies. It is also worth noting that some publishers, for example Oxford University Press,

provide open access enhanced material for their texts, absorbing development costs into textbook pricing without additional charge.

There are advantages for students, course leaders and institutions in the use of digital platforms. For students, quizzes, homework questions and comprehension exercises provide instant feedback on progress. Pearson, for example, promises 'consistent, measurable gains in student learning outcomes, retention, and subsequent course success' (Pearson Publishing Ltd 2017b). For course leaders, slides, videos and lesson plans promise an easier classroom load, while access to student learning patterns and test results serves to engage with struggling students and identify course weaknesses. For institutional administrators, an overall view of courses provides a snapshot of student engagement and a prediction of student retention.

Depending on the degree of access a student has and the material available, platforms may also include access to the digital text of a entire book and/or to specific selected chapters from a range of titles as part of customised provision for a specific course. If access for all enrolled students to course-specific resources has been purchased by the university, the platform is likely to be embedded or wrapped into the university's VLE, providing single log-on access to students, a smooth transition which enables learning.

There are, of course, issues with digital platforms beyond cost, notably the reliance on digital text which, as discussed, promotes a scan-and-skim learning style. There are also privacy concerns, with student analytics available to a number of University staff, and particularly, to platform vendors, who can then use that information to upsell further products or for their own development strategies (Raths 2018), or indeed, sell that information to any other interested party; for some EdTech suppliers, only click-through consent is required. This privacy concern is reinforced by the recent acknowledgement from Pearson that the publisher had been experimenting on students enrolled on their platforms without student knowledge or consent (Strauss 2018): Pearson has a development strategy of rolling out platforms free to a few schools, using the resulting data for development and then charging for access (Rheingold 2015).

With this corporate, commodified textual market highly visible to students, bookshops, librarians and academics, it is hardly surprising that institutions are working towards alternative models of textual provision

beyond the repurposing of the rental and second-hand markets. Open access textbooks and New University Presses, for example, have developed from this milieu, and these options are not the only opportunities in alternative textbook publication, both digital and physical. It is in negotiating these new models of textual provision and their markets, as well as in upholding the traditions of academic bookselling, that the future of the academic bookshop may be found.

3.4 Open Access

With student feedback an increasing influencer of textbook choice and focused on value, the pressure on educators to provide 'no added extras' courses and the increasing awareness of and interest in student equity with regards to resources, the open access textbook has become an attractive choice. It is by definition 'free', sustainable and almost always digitally available, thus eliminating the inequalities of access via student income, and aiding accessibility. In addition, text is usually flexible, allowing updating, editing and formatting without copyright issues, while students are free to print as needed. There are drawbacks. One lecturer mentioned, 'my students want to use an open access textbook, but the standard is lower than I'd expect' (Hawker 2016f). Content standards can vary, as can production and editing values. 'Free' too can vary. Some suppliers are dependent upon institutional funding (Knowledge Unlatched 2018) or pay-to-publish fees; for some open access purveyors, the text is free, but additional resources for academics and students are costly (Flat World Knowledge 2018). If the text is accessed online, there can be privacy concerns, and for those concerned with ethical issues, the labour involved in creating and servicing open access text is seldom acknowledged. Dr Chris Sangwin's acclaimed STACK online assignment package, designed as an open access digital learning resource along the lines of Cengage's WebAssign, is the result of a personal project; while author and publisher David Diez laughed, for example, when queried about servicing his highly successful open access textbooks, and said that management involved 'a lot of volunteer labor'.

For academic bookshops the adoption of an open access textbook is not a threat but an opportunity. While it is unlikely – but not impossible – that

many academic bookshops will be involved in hosting open access digital text, far more likely to be linked from or wrapped within the course VLE, ordering, importing, printing and stocking that open access text as physical copy has proved to be a valuable use of shop expertise in sourcing copies and of stock capital. Students, still committed to physical text, are grateful for the ease of purchase; course leaders appreciate the availability of learning resources; and sales often match or surpass those for conventional textbooks for the same course.

David Diez's OpenIntro Statistics texts provide an example of a successful open access textbook adoption for University of Edinburgh Economics students. Access is offered via the course's VLE to the digital text, while the physical text is imported by Blackwell Edinburgh. As a POD title shipped from the United States, provision has to be carefully managed, but ethical considerations by the publisher resulted in a price to students for physical copy, even with shipping costs, of £7.99 – £8.99 per text. Take-up rates approached a remarkably popular 75 per cent for this student body: the previous textbook for this course, then priced at £45.99, had average take-up rates of 32 per cent (Hawker 2014–18).

Another successful adoption has been the popular Oxford University Press CORE Economics textbook. An open access text produced to support the radical UCL-based Curriculum Open-access Resource for Economics project, it is available as free digital text and as paid-for physical text. Printed just in time for students starting a first-year economics course at Manchester in September 2017, the £39.99 physical book startled publisher, bookshop and course leaders with a 66 per cent take-up among the student body.

With open access text development fuelled by public and private investment, and attractive to educators and students alike, adoption rates are likely to increase as better-fit texts become available to educators. For bookshops, tracking and supporting those adoptions is vital: the adopter of *OpenIntro Statistics* was initially doubtful that students would be interested in physical copy while digital copy was free. This conviction was dispelled.

3.5 Personalised Text

The 'do it yourself' attitude which creates open access text can be thematically slotted into the increasing characterisation of learning resources as personal – personalised aids to study. Allison Bailey of BCG commented in 2014 that 'companies such as Flat World Knowledge have lower cost structures and often more flexible delivery options than traditional publishers. They offer customization tools to "build your own textbook" from a variety of pre-existing and newly created content' (Bailey *et al.* 2014). Personalisation is also a prominent sales strategy of the world's largest academic publisher. Pearson, investing heavily in automated learning and artificial intelligence, on a webpage personalised for New York educators, comments, 'we believe the future of American education and the path to improved student outcomes comes through personalized learning models – for students, educators, schools, and districts' (Pearson Publishing Ltd 2018c). Perceived wisdom suggests that learning models are becoming inclusive, life-long and far from the image of a typical full-time undergraduate student: MOOC tracker Course Central, for example, reports 81 million students undertaking MOOCs in 2017 (Shah 2017), although the fall in part-time study in the UK – 56 per cent in six years (Universities UK 2017) – engenders considerable concern among educators. Peter Horrocks of the Open University commented in 2017, '[S]tudents who have been most deterred from study by that huge potential debt are not "young students" whom the prime minister championed, but older, especially disadvantaged students' (Horrocks 2017).

For the bookshop, the opportunities created by evolving POD technology (Wilson-Higgins 2017), personalised digital learning resources and open access text can and should be embraced. Successful Parisian bookshop La Librairie des Puf, for example, carries virtually no physical stock but has production rights to three million–plus titles and an Espresso printing machine. Production takes, they estimate, five minutes. US EdTech company XanEdu has built a business model around providing physical and digital learning resources, often open access, always course-specific. In the UK, Ingram-owned Lightning Source claims and often achieves a POD turnaround of 48 hours per title, order to delivery. Although early

bookshop investment in POD technology was not successful – Blackwell Charing Cross returned their Espresso printing machine in 2010, citing unreliable production and insufficient demand – the infrastructure for outsourcing printing is robust and the demand for physical text continuing. In these circumstances, the capacity of the bookshop to collaborate with their institution, providing flexible physical text, supporting individual courses, while removing the burden of organisation and distribution from the university, is both a viable and potentially profitable option.

This is effectively the case for Blackwell Edinburgh, working with the custom Global Management Series titles for Heriot Watt University. To take one title as an example, Robert MacIntosh and Kevin D. O'Gorman's *Introducing Management in a Global Context* is a POD custom title created specifically for "Management in a Global Context" students. The title requires some negotiation and time investment from the bookshop in equipping students: distribution has to be on campus and via courier for domestic and international distance learners; the book must be available physically, digitally and in a physical/digital pack, and as both a bulk institutional purchase and an individual purchase. Extensive consultation between bookshop, authors, course leaders, librarians, publisher and supplier was needed to ensure successful delivery. Take-up rates for year one, personal purchase, physical or physical/digital copy, were 35 per cent: for year two, including second-hand copies, 65 per cent.

3.6 Learning Analytics

Oversight has become an ongoing theme in TEF-related textual investment. Digital text supplier Kortext, for example, argues that the product it supplies is not text, but analytics. Working in partnership with Microsoft, Kortext analytics measure student engagement with text via time spent reading and when that reading takes place, page count and active learning response to enhanced features such as notes taken and bookmarks made (Nicora 2018). Access to the analytics dashboard is scalable, so that a lecturer can access data for their own students, while a university administrator can access analytics across the university. Analytical data, Kortext claims, aids in student retention, enabling lecturers to pinpoint students struggling with course material,

and in course evaluation, allowing administrators to rank student engagement by course across the university. Student retention is, not co-incidentally in terms of Kortext's development aims, one of the metrics involved in the TEF awards. More widely, in concentrating on technological rather than textual supply and on marketing itself as an investment for venture capital, Kortext positions itself not as an academic bookshop, but as a creator of educational technology – EdTech.

The advantages and disadvantages of learning analytics have been discussed above, as well as the advantages to a local academic bookshop of collaborating with an EdTech company which can provide analytic services alongside digital text, in partnership with the bookshop's supply of physical text. However, there are other options for academic bookshops, students and course leaders, both low and high tech.

The first option is the surprising amount of information available to booksellers when looking at ordinary physical book sales. This information, proactively shared with course leaders on a timely basis and reflecting actual as well as reported student choices, can inform decision-making on a yearly basis. While the most basic information available is adoption or sell-through rates – the proportion of students on a course purchasing a new or second-hand textbook – there are other metrics which can support bookshop, students and course leader. For example:

(i) A pattern of continued high sales beyond the first rush of the start of semester suggests a text which is useful and popular among students, a peer-group recommendation and a highly successful adoption.

(ii) Poor sales and early returns suggest a text which is a poor fit for the course: tactful investigation of alternative recommendations may be useful.

(iii) High, late sales for an open-book exam course book suggest that information was not fully communicated to students: late purchasers may well be disadvantaged when it comes to that exam. Some late sales are inevitable. Many are worrisome.

(iv) High physical sales for a digital text provided by the institution – open access or paid for – would suggest that the institution may well find it worthwhile to consider offering either physical or digital options, or both formats.

(v) The sales pattern of medical texts – low in the first week or two of term, increasing in weeks three and four – is highly suggestive of purchased or pirated digital text, followed by physical text purchase, a surmise validated by gentle questioning. This observation informed the open access strategy mentioned above.

(vi) Letting course leaders know about second-hand purchase timetables can inform both the sending of a reminder to take used textbooks to the bookshop and a mention to new students that second-hand books are available. This kind of collaboration can also inform booksellers about students who should be holding onto a textbook for future study, or courses where older editions are acceptable for student use and can be bought back and sold on.

The second option, far more speculative at the moment for UK supply but already in use elsewhere, is to combine the popular advantages of physical text with the resources and analytics of digital learning resources. Printer CTPS, based in Hong Kong, initially conceived the Phygitalbook for publisher Marshall Cavendish as a response to physical book piracy, but further development offers a successful physical/digital hybrid. Each book has a unique code allowing registration and access to digital resources, which are consequently available via QR codes on the printed page. For students, this combination of physical and digital text allows a preferred and personalised learning style; for publishers, resources are both available and protected against both physical and digital piracy, while course leaders have access to both teaching resources and learner use analytics. From the bookshop's point of view this option allows the best of both worlds to student and course leader. Though these options are not yet available in the UK, Hong Kong publishers serving the Chinese market are increasingly providing hybrid text – for example, Beluga Printers, providing Super QR coding.

3.7 Dynamic Marketing and Pricing

Relevant to themes of personalisation, privacy and equity are the bookshop's options for both marketing and pricing. Dynamic marketing is effectively in place already for many bookshops utilising, for example, a list of social

science lecturers or of students interested in quantitative research, which may or may not be aided by a loyalty card linked to purchases. More invasive analysis such as that utilised by Amazon (amazon.co.uk 2018a) can list every title viewed online as well as every title bought, purchase patterns, or predict that if a student purchases Craig's *EU Law* in September they are likely to need *Blackstone's EU Treaties & Legislation* in March. Traditional book-sellers may not only recognise individual customers but purchase stock to their tastes and then recommend those titles, as well as buying around the subject areas of their university.

There are both advantages and disadvantages to the bookshop in collecting and utilising personal data. Obviously, data has to be legal, collected with the active agreement of the person involved and securely stored, compliant with the requirements of both local personal data protection laws and, in the UK and EU, the General Data Protection Regulation (GDPR) (Information Commissioner's Office 2018a). In some cases, for example, in the maintenance of reading list information, personal data retention and use comes under the legitimate interests portion of the GDPR (Information Commissioner's Office 2018b), but the reuse of that data for marketing purposes alone – for example, emailing lecturers about a Lonely Planet spring promotion – would be a risky and debatable legitimate interest use, unless the lecturer has already actively agreed to general emails from the bookshop. In terms of dynamic online advertising – for example, adverts for a particular publisher's business textbook catalogue tied to key word searches for 'marketing textbook' – there is yet to be a test case under GDPR, and it could be argued that tagged searches do not involve personal information but rather a device's address. Admittedly, few bricks-and-mortar academic bookshops have either the interest or resources for such a widespread advertising campaign, but for publishers and EdTech companies this is a viable option.

The issue of dynamic pricing also has its roots in existing, low-tech options, developing into personalised hi-tech provision. For example, as already discussed, many academic bookshops already offer differentiated pricing with price matching for students, university staff discounts or reciprocal benefits for local companies and employees. The benefits may be duplicated online: Amazon, for example, offers additional benefits to

students enrolling as student prime members, which involves divulging information about their institutions and areas of study, enabling personalised dynamic pricing – students could benefit from deals on books covering their subject area, for example, but Amazon also has the capacity to hike prices for that person in that subject area (Amazon.co.uk 2018c). With similar automation creeping into academic bookshops – stock terminals have been available for customers for at least two decades, self-service checkouts are common for big box retailers stocking text, smart shelf prices are possible if not yet adopted in the UK – personal pricing has already been utilised by Amazon at its bricks-and-mortar bookstores in the United States, where books are charged to a customer's account and recommendations can be sent to the customer's device while they are in-store (Soper 2016).

Dynamic pricing via whatever method may benefit both customer and bookshop, rewarding loyalty for both parties, but issues of morality have disturbed some booksellers concerned about equitable outreach to all customers.

3.8 Sustainability and Equity

With the student experience being the keystone of current provision for students, and with universities – and bookshops – concerned with ethical issues and learning resources, sustainability and equity have proved to be key words in text supply. There is a certain degree of irony in highlighting these components of an academic bookshop's strategy while also discussing dynamic pricing and the continuing popularity of physical text, but these options are not incompatible. Communication, when it comes to these emotive issues, in a community where pastoral care has become central to student well-being, is vital (Minsky 2016).

The academic bookshop in particular faces two related ethical issues for which an effective counterargument is vital. Both are issues of real concern to students and educators; both have been very effectively co-opted by learning resource providers, deflecting criticism towards the bookshop, or perhaps the campus bookstore, for both arguments originate from the United States.

The first issue is evident to any bookseller talking to students: the bookshop is the customer-facing end of the textual supply chain. As such, customers understandably feel that it is the bookshop which is responsible

for text pricing. Christopher Dawson of ZDNet Education characterises purchases from bookshops as 'an absolute racket' (Dawson 2010b); Chris Aldrich suggests that universities should 'consider barring textbook sales on campus and relying on the larger competitive market to supply textbooks to students' (Aldrich 2015). And the much quoted anonymous article *Here's Exactly Why College Textbooks Are So Expensive* states as its first argument: 'half of their costs go straight to publishers and university bookstores' (attn:staff 2015). Comparative bookshop and publisher margins, and additional provision to students, have been discussed earlier, but it is worth mentioning the National Association of College Stores' then Director of PR, Charles Schmidt, who responded to Christopher Dawson with a comprehensive survey of campus bookstores' involvement with lowering prices. 'I believe you do your readers a disservice by perpetuating the common misperception that buying textbooks online is always better and always cheaper. That's just not true,' he said, and summarised how bookshops are lowering prices. Dawson was not convinced: 'From my perspective, it is time for the entire model to change' (Dawson 2010a).

This bookshop-blaming argument is exactly the position taken by the larger academic publishers. By deflecting disgust at textbook prices onto bookshops, and by taking advantage of value-driven price perception fuelled by Amazon's pricing strategy rather than their own – for the margins offered to Amazon and to campus bookshops are often the same (Hawker 2008–2018a) – publishers have colonised the moral high ground of equal provision to all students. This equal provision is to be provided at the hand of the publisher, paid for by the educational provider, and preferably provided as digital text – for it is far easier to control digital text provision than it is physical. In one stroke, therefore, the publisher eliminates the second-hand and rental markets, the discounting margins extracted by physical and online bookshops and the vagaries of student purchase, gaining complete control over student choice. And yet, commentators are persuaded this is the moral high ground. 'If inclusive access is such a great idea, why don't we just snap our fingers and make it happen?' Joseph Esposito argues in his analysis of the textbook market. He goes on to state that the obstacles to this publisher-provided equity are an institution's contract with a campus bookshop, which may be exclusive in terms of

on-campus text and is likely to offer the institution rent, sales taxes to local government and the current formatting of digital editions (Esposito 2017). Joseph Esposito is a supporter of open access text, but it does not seem to have occurred to him in his summary that an exclusive deal with the same publishers responsible for the same textbook selection and pricing strategies he castigates earlier in the same piece may not be a wholly positive experience for students. Yet this same argument is echoed with some force across the Internet, not just by the publishers themselves (McGraw-Hill Education 2017c) but by students.

Rajiv Jhangiani offers a cogent counterargument. He describes the publisher model of inclusive access as 'this sounds really great until you begin to tally the compromises that are being made on the side of student agency, academic freedom, and textbook format,' adding, 'remember that the true power of open comes not from a resource being free of cost but rather from the freedoms to reuse, retain, redistribute, revise, and remix content' (Jhangiani 2017).

For the academic bookshop, faced with institutional assumptions around pricing and provision to students, the best option is open and honest communication, structured around provision for students, cognisant of stresses and clear about options. Enabling lecturers as partners in text provision eliminates the information gap between bookshop and institution. For example, there are strong ethical arguments for a transparent and equitable online and in-store pricing strategy, for both new and second-hand books, rather than the membership-based additional discounts of, for example, Amazon Student Prime or online IP-based dynamic pricing. Honest discussion with course leaders and/or administrators, either around institutional pricing or so that bookshop prices can be communicated to students before arrival on campus, removes any uncertainty around learning material costs to institution or student, a key component of student discontent with added costs. Leeds Beckett Student Union commented, '[H]idden fees mean that University enrolment is not an open process as it fails to provide a true and honest assessment of the cost of studying' (Leeds Beckett Student Union 2018).

For students purchasing their own text, efforts to reduce costs are now attractive not only to students themselves but to course leaders. Second-hand supply is a key feature of these efforts to reduce costs, and should be

a cornerstone of a bookshop's community involvement, not just for the bookshop's own sales but as a responsible partner within the university's sustainability policy. Unlike digital text, ownership of physical text can be transferred, and with courses increasingly semesterised and visiting international students often on campus for a single semester, purchasing and selling second-hand copies becomes not only supportive of students and a useful sales strategy but an environmental imperative. Blackwell Edinburgh's on-campus involvement with second-hand text, for example, was given fresh emphasis by a meeting with the University's property department, concerned with textbooks abandoned in university accommodation. As the bookshop already donated unsalable textbooks and had a policy of recommending alternative vendors to students where needed, the bookshop was ideally placed to help out. This meeting led to an agreement with the student union to promote all forms of physical text recycling across campus, from utilising the student-run recycling hub SHRUB, through personal online book selling, to the bookshop itself: second-hand sales increased by 30 per cent in a year, while SHRUB, Amnesty, Barnados and Better World Books also benefitted. In year two this successful information campaign was rolled out to all higher education providers in Edinburgh.

In terms of a single course with an assigned textbook, contacting lecturers about readoptions for first and second semester in time for second-hand sales and purchases at the end of each semester not only aids the bookshop with early adoption information, and the acceptability of older editions, but aids course leaders as they communicate with students. Contacting lecturers prior to course commencement with information about second-hand stock levels and prime buying periods also helps.

For some bookshops, a second-hand offer is a straightforward payment from bookshop to student: Blackwell, for example, currently offers 33.33 per cent of a book's RRP as a debit or credit payment, or 40 per cent as shop credit; John Smith's, 33 per cent in cash, or up to 50 per cent as credit. Others act as a proxy seller, keeping accounts for students. Crossways, a smaller independent, estimates sales of second-hand books at £18,000 in 2016; for a larger academic bookshop, sales can be proportionately higher. Equally important is the help the bookshop offers and is seen to offer for students and the environment.

Environmentally friendly use of text would suggest offering all students digital text rather than physical, although the perception that digital text has less impact than physical is not entirely true. The resources needed to produce a single printed book are undoubtedly more destructive that those used to create an e-book, but the use of resources in the manufacture of a device used to read the e-book have considerably more impact, particularly in the use of nonrenewable rare mineral resources. The Green Press Initiative, itself quoting studies by Daniel Goleman and Gregory Norris and by Cleantech, for example, estimates an environmental cost per physical book of 8.85 pounds of carbon dioxide per book sold, while an iPad is responsible for 287 pounds of carbon dioxide and a Kindle 370 pounds, equivalent respectively to between forty and seventy physical books; although 'in terms of impacts on human health, 1 E-book has 70 times the impact of 1 printed book, with the primary impact being particulate matter from energy use and production' (Green Press Initiative 2015). Michael Carter, writing for the Eco Guide in favour of e-books, suggests both an eco-footprint for a physical book of 7.5 kg and that this is the equivalent of twenty-two e-books, stating, 'reading over 44 books on an e-reader would actually halve a person's impact on the climate' and that 'eBooks clearly have the potential to lessen CO2 emissions. That being said, it is important to take in all facets of the books vs. eBooks debate as well as look at possible alternatives, like libraries and apps' (Carter 2015). It is possible to argue, therefore, that the environmental impact of a given format depends on a student's use of that format, with library supply of physical books considerably less destructive than the provision of five or six essential e-books and a device on which to read them to each student, but for a research student accessing multiple texts a personal device has a far smaller environmental footprint.

It is vital to note, though, that for some students digital text is not a choice but the only way in which they can access printed educational material. Adaptable technology as applied to text-based learning resources has enabled student participation across the world, and for all academic publishers provision of that access may be a moral imperative, but is almost certainly, in the major digital marketplaces, a legal imperative as well. In the UK, for example, 'Under the Equality Act 2010, education and training

providers and other related services have a duty to make reasonable adjustments for disabled people so they are not placed at a substantial disadvantage compared to non-disabled students' (Disability Rights UK 2017). This encompasses the provision of accessible text, both through a course-specific VLE and through the academic library when needed for personal research. In response, all major and most minor academic publishers have a specific department or person responsible for supplying accessible digital text. For these students, digital resources are not a choice but a necessity, and any textbook strategy – bookshop, educator, publisher – should encompass enabling access rather than restricting it.

As universities widen their remit to include students who would not previously have been able to enroll in further and higher education, the academic bookshop has a role to play. Enabling physical access to text by adapting the environment of the bricks-and-mortar bookshop with wider aisles, accessible signage, ramps and lower counters (Walker 2015) is an obvious and often mandated adaption, but there are more considerations than physical access. The traditional academic bookshop – dark, filled with stacks of books, staffed by specialists – can be intimidating to some students, an issue brought home by recent debate in the bookselling community around WHSmith. An article in the *Spectator* described the bookseller as a 'national embarrassment' due to its shabby stores and poor range of books (Butterfield 2016), while readers voted it the 'UK's worst high street shop' (Thomson 2018). CEO Steve Clarke gave a robust defence (Armstrong 2017), but perhaps most telling was the plethora of readers and writers who defended WHSmith's appeal to people who felt uncomfortable in traditional bookshops. Author Joanne Harris, for example, said, 'while it may not be the coolest shop on the High Street, research suggests that W H Smith, and not Waterstone's, is the place where most working-class people buy books. If we care at all about promoting literacy, we should at least be aware of this' (Onwuemezi 2018a).

If the academic bookshop is invested in promoting text, then the onus is on the bookshop to promote a welcoming environment for all students. The Bookseller's Association is currently running a diversity initiative which would allow academic bookshops to invest in recruitment, training and outreach (Bookseller's Association 2018), and many universities now

also have outreach programmes with which the bookshop can align themselves. Bookshops like Nottingham's Five Leaves, a successful independent closely aligned with the university's teaching staff, have a diverse events programme, inclusive title ranges and an overt agenda of radical and inclusive bookselling as part of the community they serve. Five Leaves itself was the British Book Awards Independent Bookshop of the Year in 2018. Publisher and bookseller Sharmaine Lovegrove commented, 'if you don't have a diverse workforce or product, sooner or later you won't exist' (Lovegrove 2018), and for academic bookshops, serving an increasingly diverse community, her words carry an evident truth, as the bookshop traverses the intersections of privilege and inclusion.

For some institutions and students budgetary constraints are so severe that innovative solutions must be sought in order to access academic text. For example, in 2015–17, following consolidation, the newly constituted Edinburgh College had no budget for physical text. In consequence, during this period, the college's schools, informatics team, and library worked together to create their innovative in-house VLEs, in which every piece of text is either internally produced or open access. This period was exceptionally difficult for some course leaders, however, who depended on students having access to commercially produced text and resources. Here, bookshop, publisher and course leaders worked together to lower the cost of text supplied to students at discount: a combination of bespoke offer, stalls and dedicated online material has served to equip students for learning.

In addition to supporting institutions, in a social contribution which also helps embed the bookshop within their community, bookshops can also leverage their purchasing power to pressure publishers into supplying text and resources for students receiving hardship grants, a welcome offer for lecturers who are increasingly involved in pastoral care and vital to the students themselves. Bookshops have also passed information about legal online access to necessary text to lecturers. For example, after Jurafsky's *Speech and Language Processing* went from an RRP of £58.99 in 2016 to one of £146.67 in 2017, booksellers at Blackwell South Bridge publicised access to the online version as well as offering a second-hand sourcing service which equipped all students desiring physical text – and still held the book

in stock, since some students were prepared to pay the new price for a pristine copy.

3.9 Collaboration

Sourcing copies of Jurafsky for students was a collaboration which required bookshop, booksellers, course leaders and students to work together. Not only did this collaboration pay dividends for the bookshop in terms of increased trust and social capital, it built on and added to a portfolio of collaboration which serves to embed an academic bookshop within the community it serves, in the same way that a successful general bookshop tailors its stock, events and outreach to the community within which it is based.

At the most basic level for an academic bookshop, accurate information on courses, course leaders, titles and student numbers is essential to the provision of learning resources, whether to offer institutional purchase, to order and market titles for student purchase or to select supporting subject-adjacent text. Year-on-year information allows analysis of stock, purchase trends and investigation of pricing implications over time. Additional information is vital to the success of provision for students: for example, the seminar timing of a multi-text foreign language course, the date of an open book exam or the use of a lecturer's own book. It is equally essential that a course leader be provided with information that may impact on accessibility: a reprinting or an out-of-print title, or a rights issue which means a title may not be available in the UK. For many academic book-shops, sharing information and collaborating with their university libraries is equally essential.

For some courses and course leaders, extra provisions may be useful: supporting the adoption of open access text, on-site stalls for student purchase of highly recommended text, mitigating the impact of temporarily unavailable text and supplying course leaders with sell-through rates for both successful and unsuccessful material. Individual texts can be supported online with customised pages and social media support, an effective counter to other online providers. This kind of personalised service is far easier for a campus-based bricks-and-mortar bookshop than for a centralised online provider – see, for example, Kortext's partnerships with John Smith's and

Blackwell's – but can be time consuming. Increasing automation and ease of data manipulation may lift some of the burden and eventually replace person-to-person communication for many courses, in the same way, for example, that automated purchase is built into the Talis or Leganto reading list websites for university libraries.

Collaboration between academic bookshop and academic community can go far beyond textual provision. Some of the more exciting projects involving the academic bookshop are the production and distribution of new academic texts, whether through a university press or through a one-off project. For new or small publishers, booksellers can provide professional consultation on issues of pricing, of distribution and of marketing, exactly the sort of advice respondents to JISC's *Changing Publisher Ecologies* New University Press survey (Adema 2016) were hoping to

Figure 4. Promotion and Research

Promotional leaflet for course textbooks alongside text use research survey. Image © Blackwell UK/James Anderson, used by permission.

receive. For textbooks, bookshops provide an easy and efficient means of providing students with their books through institutional or student purchase – every single publisher involved in JISC's *Institution as e-textbook Publisher* (JISC 2015), for example, published physical as well as digital versions of their text, and almost all depended on direct rather than institutional purchase. Booksellers are also well equipped to assess the potential for book proposals, both for general and custom publication, assessing options and referring academics to publishers.

This deep understanding of academic bookselling, of textbooks and of the academic community, can be utilised by course leaders. Academic bookshops have given presentations to marketing students, represented local industries on business courses, and sat on public panels and discussions around bookselling for legislative and local interest. Academic booksellers have written papers and monographs, presented at conferences, and both written and responded to commentary in local, national and online reporting – a profile which also serves to reinforce respect for a local bookshop within their academic community. As mentioned, it is reportedly due to John Smith's bookseller Peter Lake, for example, that the initial TEF legislation included reference to learning resources, thus enabling the institutional purchase which has supported academic bookshops and students since introduction (Lake 2016a).

There are smaller ways in which academic bookshops embed themselves into their community. Bookshops support conference and local book launches; provide study skills events; support local publishing and writing; create or offer homes to book groups and debating societies; theme stock around local issues, national debates and growth areas of study; support new learners, new writers and researchers; and support staff and retired academics with stock, advice and a friendly, informed ability to listen. Practically, especially with the high staff turnover at many academic publishers, bookshops can provide advice for students – how to access helplines for digital resources and what to say to operators, for example, has proven particularly useful information to disseminate – and for academics in terms of accessing class resources or desk copies. In addition, academic bookshops learn from their customers not only the success or otherwise of their marketing and pricing strategies, but also information on new areas of

Figure 5. Academic Bookshop, Edinburgh

Traditional academic bookshop in Edinburgh, Scotland: exterior, first lecture stall, unpacking textbooks. Photographs © J. M. Hawker

study, new books, alterations to university policy, student concerns, the efficiency of a particular textbook, gossip, complaints, compliments and jokes. An academic bookshop includes not only its stock and staff but its community.

The Future

'I didn't think where students bought their books was anything to do with me,' said a University of Edinburgh lecturer, calling their local bookshop two weeks after being warned by that bookshop that students were not purchasing text as they had done in previous years. With a new edition out, notes, exercises and solutions no longer matched the recommended text, but it had taken a while for first-year students to mention the discrepancy. The

lecturer received a copy of the new edition within twenty minutes. Within twenty-four hours they had rewritten their notes, and students were returning to the bookshop to purchase and use that text.

It would be easy to say that this anecdote illustrates the benefits of a local academic bookshop, but it encapsulates more than a simple solution to a singular issue. TEF, the NSS and the increasing use of internal student feedback have meant that academic teaching staff has taken on responsibilities beyond the traditional tasks, and the provision of learning resources is now perceived by students to be part of those responsibilities, whether through direct or indirect provision. There is pressure from students and management to provide financially and environmentally sustainable, and equitable, access to text, and that access is now governed by legislation as well as institutional and academic preference. For the local academic bookshop, these are legal and social responsibilities not just central to the successful provision of academic text, but specialist selling points. As a native inhabitant of the textual marketplace, the knowledgeable academic bookseller can offer proactive and thoughtful solutions to their institutions and academics – sometimes before the institution or academic is aware that those solutions are needed.

Knowledge of marketplace drivers is not enough. Publishers, booksellers, academic institutions and students are all under financial pressure. Understanding and negotiating those pressures includes, but is not limited to a simplistic financial accounting of supply chain management. In providing publisher-negotiated online and on-campus discounts for direct and indirect supply of new physical and digital text, in urging the use of sustainable and cheap second-hand text, in actively working towards equitable text access alongside libraries and hardship fund administrators, the academic bookshop is able to encompass a flexibility in price that benefits their academic community as a whole – one which also informs the sustainability of the bookshop itself.

It is knowledge too which informs decision making within the shifting ecology of the academic text. While larger academic publishers look to consolidation, smaller publishers are experimenting with new forms of creating and delivering text. Digitalisation has both consolidated and fragmented supply, as established publishers look to platform-based delivery and

embrace custom text or deconstructed formatting, while new publishers embrace new forms of text, supply, and delivery. Open access text, both as a choice and as a legal requirement, rental models and hybrid physical/digital text alongside the development of text-based resources have all impacted on the nature of academic text. Positioned between supplier and end consumer, the academic bookshop is in a unique position to evaluate the benefits and drawbacks of each model and can bring the benefit of that knowledge to their academic community.

In an age of cut-throat margins, big data, automation and the restructuring not only of the bookselling marketplace but of the nature of text, when the closure of one academic bookseller is a loss to an already small community, booksellers fear the future. But the demise of the academic bookshop has been predicted for decades, and the bookshop, online and on campus, still exists. Many are thriving. And while the establishment of a new academic bookshop can still make headlines (Littlejohns 2016), that new bookshop is built on skills and traditions of a community which has existed since the first written record was traded, encompassed the information age and is looking to the future. To devalue the academic bookshop, online or off, is to devalue the academics who can trust the curation, stock management and innovation of its buyers, the students who continue to depend on the knowledge and skill of its booksellers, and the publishers who depend on the bookshop as both academic liaison and shop window. It also underestimates the knowledge, financial skills and ingenuity of bookshop managers, negotiating discounts and bundle prices, evaluating analytics or sourcing venture capital, playing margin against quantity sales, pushing publishers to discount for students and suppliers to cut costs, providing training and support, finding opportunities and offering ingenious solutions, and maintaining the financial health of both bookshop and booksellers.

To paraphrase Alison Bailey's 2014 report on the academic publishing industry (Bailey *et al.* 2014), the academic bookshop already encompasses the skills that will master a changing marketplace: 'the industry has several advantages that it can use to transform its operating model and the way it goes to market. Many of these skills, capabilities, and assets were underappreciated in the old world of [publishing] but have become extremely valuable in a data-driven digital learning environment.'

Capital Letters summarises current opportunities and innovations for academic bookshops in a changing marketplace, and characterises new directions and services. At the same time, the traditional curatorial, knowledgeable skills of the academic bookseller are seen to be both valued and valuable: academic bookselling can learn from looking back as well as looking forward. Innovation, communication and collaboration are vital. So too is the bookseller's experience, knowledge and probity, and dedication to providing for the needs of all customers, for it is those customers – as students, as part-time booksellers themselves, as academics and as administrators, as gift or travel guide or fiction purchasers, as readers and as writers – who continue to make the academic bookshop a vital and sustainable part of the academic community.

Bibliography

Adema, Janneke & Stone, Graham. (2016). *Changing Publisher Ecologies, a Landscape Study of New University Presses and Academic-Led Publishing*. London: JISC.

Aldrich, Chris. (2015). *To Purchase, Rent, or Pirate? The Broken Economics of Textbooks in the Digital Age*. [ONLINE] Available at: https://boffo socko.com/2015/08/24/to-purchase-rent-or-pirate-the-broken-economics -of-textbooks-in-the-digital-age/. [Accessed 14 April 2018].

amazon.co.uk. (2018a). *Amazon UK Privacy Notice*. [ONLINE] Available at: www.amazon.co.uk/gp/help/customer/display.html?nodeId=502584. [Accessed 14 April 2018].

amazon.co.uk. (2018b). *amazon.co.uk History & Timeline*. [ONLINE] Available at: http://phx.corporate-ir.net/phoenix.zhtml?c=251199& p=irol-corporateTimeline. [Accessed 14 April 2018].

amazon.co.uk. (2018c). *Prime Student*. [ONLINE] Available at: www .amazon.co.uk/Amazon-Student-Free-One-Day-Delivery/b?ie=UTF8& node=2973324031. [Accessed 14 April 2018].

Anderson, Porter. (2017). *New BookMap Initiative: Trying To Chart the World Publishing Industry*. [ONLINE] Available at: https://publishingperspec tives.com/2017/10/bookmap-launched-to-size-up-world-publishing/. [Accessed 11 October 2018].

Armstrong, Ashley. (2017). *WH Smith boss opens up about mental health, coming out and the retailer's 225-year anniversary in first ever interview*. [ONLINE] Available at: www.telegraph.co.uk/business/2017/01/02/wh-smith-boss-opens-mental-health-coming-retailers-225-year/. [Accessed 14 April 2018].

Atherton, Graeme, Dumangane, Constantino, & Whitty, Geoff. (2017). *Charting Equity in Higher Education: Drawing the Global Access Map*.

[ONLINE] Available at: www.pearson.com/content/dam/one-dot-com/one-dot-com/global/Files/about-pearson/innovation/Charting-Equity_WEB.pdf. [Accessed 14 April 2018].

attn: staff. (2015). *Here's Exactly Why College Textbooks Are So Expensive.* [ONLINE] Available at: www.attn.com/stories/1164/heres-exactly-why-college-textbooks-are-so-expensive. [Accessed 14 April 2018].

Bagshaw, Ant. (2017). *A beginner's guide to the Teaching Excellence Framework.* [ONLINE] Available at: https://wonkhe.com/blogs/a-beginners-guide-to-the-teaching-excellence-framework/. [Accessed 14 April 2018].

Bailey, Allison, Davis, Peter, Henry, Tyce, & Loureiro, Kristen. (2014). *The Digital Disruption of Education Publishing, How Online Learning Is Reshaping the Industry's Ecosystem.* [ONLINE] Available at: www.bcg.com/en-gb /publications/2014/media-entertainment-digital-disruption-of-education-publishing.aspx. [Accessed 14 April 2018].

Barker, Andrew. (2015). *The University of Liverpool – 'institution as e-book creator' project with JISC* [ONLINE] Available at: http://blog.alpsp.org /2015/06/the-university-of-liverpool-institution.html. [Accessed 14 April 2018].

Baron, Naomi. (2015). *Words Onscreen: The Fate of Reading in a Digital World.* Oxford: Oxford University Press.

Barr, Christopher D., Diez, David M., & Çetinkaya-Rundel, Mine. (2011) *OpenIntro Statistics.* [ONLINE] Available at: www.openintro.org/stat/textbook.php. [Accessed 14 April 2018].

Baverstock, Alison. (1990). *How to Market Books.* London: Kogan Page

BBC. (2009). *Amazon's Kindle to launch in UK.* [ONLINE] Available at: http://news.bbc.co.uk/1/hi/technology/8294310.stm. [Accessed 14 April 2018].

Beckett, Andy. (2009). *You can't be serious.* [ONLINE] Available at: www .ourdailyread.com/2009/05/you-cant-be-serious/. [Accessed 14 April 2018].

Belshaw, Doug. (2016). *Open Educational Thinking*. [ONLINE] Available at: https://dougbelshaw.com/blog/2016/02/11/pearson-open-badges/. [Accessed 14 April 2018].

Bennett, Linda & Bennett, Annika. (2017). *Resource Provision in Higher Education, Implications of the TEF and related initiatives*. Barnsley: Gold Leaf.

Benson-Armer, Richard, Sarakatsannis, Jimmy, & Wee, Ken. (2014). *The future of textbooks*. [ONLINE] Available at: www.mckinsey.com/industries/social-sector/our-insights/the-future-of-textbooks. [Accessed 14 April 2018].

Bookseller's Association. (2018). *The Diversity & Inclusiveness Grants (DIG) Project*. [ONLINE] Available at: www.booksellers.org.uk/industryinfo/industryinfo/Creating-Inclusive-Bookshops. [Accessed 14 April 2018].

Britain, Sandy & Liber, Oleg. (1999). *A Framework for Pedagogical Evaluation of Virtual Learning Environments*. Bangor: University of Wales.

Buckley, Chris. (2015). *China Warns Against 'Western Values' in Imported Textbooks*. [ONLINE] Available at: https://sinosphere.blogs.nytimes.com/2015/01/30/china-warns-against-western-values-in-imported-textbooks/. [Accessed 14 April 2018].

Butterfield, David. (2016). *WH Smith has become a national embarrassment*. [ONLINE] Available at: https://life.spectator.co.uk/2016/12/wh-smith-become-national-embarrassment/. [Accessed 14 April 2018].

Cambridge University Press. (2017). *Statement regarding content in The China Quarterly*. [ONLINE] Available at: www.cambridge.org/about-us/media/press-releases/cambridge-university-press-statement-regarding-content-china-quarterly. [Accessed 14 April 2018].

Cambridge University Press. (2018). *Cambridge University Press India*. [ONLINE] Available at: www.cambridgeindia.org/. [Accessed 14 April 2018].

Campbell, Lisa. (2011). *Belfast university bookshop to close.* [ONLINE] Available at: www.thebookseller.com/news/belfast-university-bookshop-close. [Accessed 14 April 2018].

Campbell, Lisa. (2016a). *APS Awards triumph for OUP, John Smiths and Blackwell's.* [ONLINE] Available at: www.thebookseller.com/news/aps-awards-triumph-oup-john-smith-and-blackwell-s-324728. [Accessed 14 April 2018].

Campbell, Lisa. (2016b). *BA backs campus bookshops as Leicester axes academic offer.* [ONLINE] Available at: www.thebookseller.com/news/ba-backs-campus-bookshops-leicester-axes-academic-offer-388186. [Accessed 14 April 2018].

Campbell, Lisa. (2016c). *Blackwell Learning acquired by Kortext.* [ONLINE] Available at: www.thebookseller.com/news/blackwell-learning-acquired-kortext-689376. [Accessed 14 April 2018].

Campbell, Lisa. (2016d). *Blackwell's trials new 'enhanced' bookshop concepts.* [ONLINE] Available at: www.thebookseller.com/news/concept-and-coffee-central-blackwell-s-campus-openings-394091. [Accessed 14 April 2018].

Campbell, Lisa. (2016e). *Publishing chiefs urged to work on bookshop floor.* [ONLINE] Available at www.thebookseller.com/news/publishing-chiefs-urged-spend-day-bookshop-floor-391791 [Accessed 14 April 2018].

Campbell, Lisa. (2016f). *University Bookseller, Plymouth closes after 42 years.* [ONLINE] Available at: www.thebookseller.com/news/university-bookseller-plymouth-closes-after-42-years-319480. [Accessed 14 April 2018].

Campbell, Lisa. (2017a). *Blackwell's 2016 financial results reflect 'challenging' year.* [ONLINE] Available at: www.thebookseller.com/news/blackwells-financial-results-relfect-challenging-year-511356. [Accessed 14 April 2018].

Campbell, Lisa. (2017b). *European Court rules e-book VAT cannot be reduced.* [ONLINE] Available at: www.thebookseller.com/news/european-

court-rules-e-book-vat-cannot-be-reduced-500211. [Accessed 14 April 2018].

Campbell, Lisa. (2018a). *Academic publishing chiefs urged to work in campus bookshops*. [ONLINE] Available at: www.thebookseller.com/news/academic-publishing-chiefs-urged-work-bookshops-784451. [Accessed 14 April 2018].

Campbell, Lisa. (2018b). *Blackwell's sales surge 12%*. [ONLINE] Available at: www.thebookseller.com/news/blackwells-sees-sales-soar-12–755771. [Accessed 14 April 2018].

Campbell, Lisa. (2018c). *JS Group hails 'positive' year as online sales grow*. [ONLINE] Available at: www.thebookseller.com/news/js-group-hails-positive-year-online-sales-grow-731022. [Accessed 14 April 2018].

Carter, Michael. (2015). *Books vs ebooks: Protect the environment with this simple decision*. [ONLINE] Available at: https://theecoguide.org/books-vs-ebooks-protect-environment-simple-decision. [Accessed 14 April 2018].

Cengage. (2017). *Cengage Learning's Course360 Provides Rich Online Course Experience*. [ONLINE] Available at: https://news.cengage.com/higher-education/cengage-learnings-course360-provides-rich-online-course-experience/. [Accessed 14 April 2018].

Centre for Competition Policy (2008). An evaluation of the impact upon productivity of ending resale price maintenance on books. [ONLINE] http://publications.aston.ac.uk/18472/1/Evaluation_of_the_impact_upon_productivity_of_ending_resale_price_maintenance_on_books.pdf [Accessed 11 October 2018].

Centre for Economics and Business Research. (2017). *Bookselling Britain: The economic contributions to – and impacts on – the economy of the UK's bookselling sector. A report for the Bookseller's Association*.

Chuck, Brad. (2017). *Academia and the University of Westminster*. [ONLINE] Available at: https://universitybusiness.co.uk/Article/aca

demia-and-the-university-of-westminster-1510225388. [Accessed 14 April 2018].

Claypoole, Cheryl. (2018). *What Is the Markup Percentage for Retail Clothing?* [ONLINE] Available at: https://smallbusiness.chron.com/markup-percentage-retail-clothing-80777.html. [Accessed 14 April 2018].

College Board. (2018). *Average Estimated Undergraduate Budgets, 2017–18, College Board Report 2017–18.* [ONLINE] Available at: https://trends.collegeboard.org/college-pricing/figures-tables/aver age-estimated-undergraduate-budgets-2017–18. [Accessed 14 April 2018].

College Scholarships. (2017). *College Textbook Scholarships.* [ONLINE] Available at: www.collegescholarships.org/scholarships/student-books.htm. [Accessed 14 April 2018].

Conlon, Gavan, Ladher, Rohit, & Halterbeck, Maike. (2017). *The determinants of international demand for UK higher education.* [ONLINE] Available at: www.hepi.ac.uk/wp-content/uploads/2017/01/Hepi-Report-91-Screen.pdf. [Accessed 14 April 2018].

Cote, Denise (2014) *United States* v. *Apple Inc.* [ONLINE] Available at: https://ia800206.us.archive.org/27/items/gov.uscourts.nysd.394628/gov .uscourts.nysd.394628.113.0.pdf [Accessed 11 October 2018].

Cowdrey, Katherine. (2017a). *JS Group reports 6% revenue drop for 2016.* [ONLINE] Available at: www.thebookseller.com/news/js-group-report-e-book-surge-despite-declines-he-496306. [Accessed 14 April 2018].

Cowdrey, Katherine. (2017b). *Pearson announces further cost cuts ahead of agm.* [ONLINE] Available at: www.thebookseller.com/news/pearson-announces-further-cost-cuts-ahead-agm-547556. [Accessed 14 April 2018].

Cowdrey, Katherine. (2018). *IPA protest HK bookseller's second kidnapping.* [ONLINE] Available at: www.thebookseller.com/news/ipa-protest-hk -publisher-kidnapping-not-spy-novel-715371.[Accessed 14 April 2018].

Cowdrey, Katherine & Campbell, Lisa. (2016). *E-books can be sold with reduced VAT, says EC*. [ONLINE] Available at: www.thebookseller.com /news/fep-and-eibf-welcome-ec-decision-reduce-vat-e-books-441101. [Accessed 14 April 2018].

Crossick, Geoffrey. (2015). *Monographs and open access A report to HEFCE*. [ONLINE] Available at: www.hefce.ac.uk/pubs/rereports/year/2015/ monographs/. [Accessed 14 April 2018].

Crossways. (2018). *Second-hand Policy*. [ONLINE] Available at: www .ma.rhul.ac.uk/files/Website%20library.pdf. [Accessed 14 April 2018].

Dadds, Craig. (2016). Back to the Future: the Role of the Campus Bookshop. In R. Lyons and S. Rayner, eds., *The Academic Book of the Future*, Basingstoke: Palgrave. Macmillan, pp. 98–103.

Daniel, David & Jakobsen, Krisztina. (2018). *E-textbooks Effectiveness Studied*. [ONLINE] Available at: www.psyc.jmu.edu/ug/features/etext books.html. [Accessed 14 April 2018].

Dawson, Christopher. (2010a). *My textbook rant: The college bookstore people respond*. [ONLINE] Available at: www.zdnet.com/article/my-textbook -rant-the-college-bookstore-people-respond/. [Accessed 14 April 2018].

Dawson, Christopher. (2010b). *The textbook racket*. [ONLINE] Available at: www.zdnet.com/article/the-textbook-racket/. [Accessed 14 April 2018].

Department for Education. (2017a). *Teaching Excellence and Student Outcomes Framework: analysis of metrics flags*. [ONLINE] Available at: https://assets.publishing.service.gov.uk/government/uploads/sys tem/uploads/attachment_data/file/651162/TEF-analysis_of_metrics_ flags.pdf. [Accessed 14 April 2018].

Department for Education. (2017b). *Teaching Excellence and Student Outcomes Framework Specification*. [ONLINE] Available at: https://assets .publishing.service.gov.uk/government/uploads/system/uploads/

attachment_data/file/658490/Teaching_Excellence_and_Student_Out
comes_Framework_Specification.pdf. [Accessed 14 April 2018].

Disability Rights UK. (2017). *Adjustments for disabled students*. [ONLINE]
Available at: www.disabilityrightsuk.org/adjustments-disabled-
students. [Accessed 14 April 2018].

Dunn, Jennifer. (2016). *Sales Tax by State: In Which States are Textbooks
Tax Exempt?* [ONLINE] Available at: https://blog.taxjar.com/text
books-tax-exempt-sales-tax/. [Accessed 14 April 2018].

Dunn, Jennifer. (2018). *Sales Tax by State: Should You Charge Sales Tax on
Digital Products?* [ONLINE] Available at: https://blog.taxjar.com
/sales-tax-digital-products/. [Accessed 14 April 2018].

Edgecliffe-Johnson, Andrew & Sender, Henry. (2013). *Cengage files for
bankruptcy protection*. [ONLINE] Available at: www.ft.com/content/
adfadcf0-e34e-11e2-bd87-00144feabdc0. [Accessed 14 April 2018].

Equality Challenge Unit. (2010). *Disability legislation: practical guidance
for academic staff*. [ONLINE] Available at: www.ecu.ac.uk/wp-content
/uploads/external/disability-legislation-for-academics-revised.pdf.
[Accessed 14 April 2018].

Elsevier. (2018). *Expert Consult from Elsevier*. [ONLINE] Available at:
https://expertconsult.inkling.com/. [Accessed 14 April 2018].

Esposito, Joseph. (2017). *How to Reduce the Cost of College Textbooks*.
[ONLINE] Available at: https://scholarlykitchen.sspnet.org/2017/
03/27/reduce-cost-college-textbooks. [Accessed 14 April 2018].

Evans, Benedict. (2014). Why Amazon Has No Profits (And Why It
Works). [ONLINE] www.ben-evans.com/benedictevans/2014/9/4/
why-amazon-has-no-profits-and-why-it-works. [Accessed 11 October
2018].

Evans, Rachel & Meadows, Jack. (1984). *Bookselling in Higher Education*.
British National Library Bibliography Research Fund Report 15.
Oxford: Elsevier.

Fazackerley, Anna. (2018). *Vice-chancellors urge action to stop predicted 60% fall in EU students*. [ONLINE] Available at: www.theguardian.com/education/2018/apr/24/vice-chancellors-urge-action-eu-students-international-fees. [Accessed 14 April 2018].

Flat World Knowledge. (2018). Open Access *Textbooks*. [ONLINE] Available at: https://catalog.flatworldknowledge.com/. [Accessed 14 April 2018].

Frost, Simon. (2015). *Bespoke bookselling for the twenty-first century: John Smith's and current UK higher education*. Bournemouth: Bournemouth University.

Frost, Simon & Hall, Stephen. (2015). *John Smith's Historical Perspectives and Historical Precedence*. [ONLINE] Available at: http://eprints.bournemouth.ac.uk/28360/1/John%20Smith%27s%20-%20Historical%20Perspectives%20and%20Historical%20Precedence%20FINAL.pdf. [Accessed 14 April 2018].

Green Press Initiative. (2015). *Environmental Impacts of E-Books*. [ONLINE] Available at: www.greenpressinitiative.org/documents/ebooks.pdf. [Accessed 14 April 2018].

Hart, Michael S. (2017). *Michael S. Hart at Project Gutenberg*. [ONLINE] Available at: www.gutenberg.org/wiki/Michael_S._Hart. [Accessed 14 April 2018].

Hawker, Jaki. (2005–18). In conversation with Palgrave, Taylor and Francis, OUP, and other publishers.

Hawker, Jaki. (2008–18a). In conversation with Taylor and Francis, Sage, Wiley, and other publishers.

Hawker, Jaki. (2008–18b). Internal sales figures, Blackwell Edinburgh.

Hawker, Jaki. (2013). Blackwell Internal Sales Review.

Hawker, Jaki. (2014–18). Internal sales figures and course records, Blackwell Edinburgh.

Hawker, Jaki (2016–18). In conversation with Taylor and Francis and Brill.

Hawker, Jaki. (2016a). In conversation with Peter Lake of JS Group.

Hawker, Jaki. (2016b). In conversation with Rebecca Heitsch of Blackwell UK.

Hawker, Jaki. (2016c). Student Review Survey 2016.

Hawker, Jaki. (2016d). In conversation with Glenn Thomas of Pearson.

Hawker, Jaki. (2016e). Internal Wiley communicaton.

Hawker, Jaki. (2016f). In conversation with University of Edinburgh Informatics Lecturers.

Hawker, Jaki. (2017a). In conversation with Blackwell Manchester manager Paul Thornton.

Hawker, Jaki. (2017b). In conversation with David Prescott of Blackwell UK.

Hawker, Jaki. (2017c). Via email with the lecturer concerned.

Hawker, Jaki. (2017d). Via conversation with the lecturer concerned.

Hawker, Jaki. (2017–18). In conversation.

Hawker, Jaki. (2018a). Internal sales reports, Blackwell UK, compiled in 2018 and relating to academic years 2016–17 and 2017–18.

Hawker, Jaki. (2018b). Blackwell stock reports for Edinburgh South Bridge and Oxford Broad Street, October 2017 & April 2018.

Hawker, Jaki. (2018c). In conversation with Fiona Anderson of Palgrave Macmillan.

Hawker, Jaki. (2018d). In conversation with John Kelly of Oxford University Press.

Hawker, Jaki. (2018e). In conversation with Kevin Watt of Kortext and Kate Stillborn of Blackwell UK.

Hawker, Jaki. (2018f). In conversation with Simon Pollard of Pearson.

Hawker, Jaki. (2018g). Internal sales reports: average turnover increase across Blackwell campus shops 4%.

Hawker, Jaki. (2018h) *Blackwell Student Survey 2018*. See Figure 2.

Hawker, Jaki. (2018i). Tracking deliveries, spring 2018.

Higher Education Funding Council for England. (2016a). *Consultation on the second Research Excellence Framework*. [ONLINE] Available at: www .hefce.ac.uk/media/HEFCE,2014/Content/Pubs/2016/201636/ HEFCE2016_36.pdf. [Accessed 14 April 2018].

Higher Education Funding Council for England. (2016b). *Open Access Research*. [ONLINE] Available at: www.hefce.ac.uk/rsrch/oa/. [Accessed 14 April 2018].

Hill, Steven. (2018a). *Open access monographs in the REF*. [ONLINE] Available at: https://blog.hefce.ac.uk/2018/02/23/open-access-monographs-ref-2027/. [Accessed 14 April 2018].

Hill, Steven. (2018b). *Redux 2018 – Session Slides and Audio Files*. [ONLINE] Available at: https://events.bizzabo.com/Redux18/page/ 1332592/slides-and-audio. [Accessed 22 May 2018].

HM Revenue & Customs. (2016). *VAT Notice 701/10: zero-rating of books and other forms of printed matter*. [ONLINE] Available at: www.gov.uk /government/publications/vat-notice-70110-zero-rating-of-books-and -other-forms-of-printed-matter/vat-notice-70110-zero-rating-of-books-and-other-forms-of-printed-matter. [Accessed 14 April 2018].

Hoffelder, Nate. (2017). *Textbook Publishers File Suit Against Amazon Marketplace Sellers for Alleged Piracy*. [ONLINE] Available at: https:// the-digital-reader.com/2017/01/24/textbook-publishers-file-suit-amazon -marketplace-sellers-alleged-piracy/. [Accessed 14 April 2018].

Horne, Alastair. (2018). *London Book Fair Academic Newsletter*. [ONLINE] Available at: http://hub.londonbookfair.co.uk/academic-newsletter-february-2018–2/. [Accessed 14 April 2018].

Horrocks, Peter. (2017). *Mature and part-time students: the real crisis of the high fees era*. [ONLINE] Available at: www.timeshighereducation.com/blog/ mature-and-part-time-students-real-crisis-high-fees-era. [Accessed 14 April 2018].

Information Commissioner's Office. (2018a). *Guide to the General Data Protection Regulation (GDPR)*. [ONLINE] Available at: https://ico .org.uk/for-organisations/guide-to-the-general-data-protection-regulation -gdpr/. [Accessed 14 April 2018].

Information Commissioner's Office. (2018b). *Rules around business to business marketing, the GDPR and PECR*. [ONLINE] Available at: https:// ico.org.uk/for-organisations/marketing/the-rules-around-business-to-business-marketing-the-gdpr-and-pecr/. [Accessed 14 April 2018].

International Publishers Association and World Intellectual Property Organization. (2018). A Pilot Survey by the IPA and WIPO The Global Publishing Industry in 2016. [ONLINE] www.wipo.int/edocs/ pubdocs/en/wipo_ipa_pilotsurvey_2016.pdf. [Accessed 11 October 2018].

Jhangiani, Rajiv. (2017). *Just how inclusive are 'inclusive access' e-textbook programs?* [ONLINE] Available at: http://thatpsychprof.com/just-how -inclusive-are-inclusive-access-programs/. [Accessed 14 April 2018].

JISC. (2015). *Institution as e-textbook Publisher*. [ONLINE] Available at: www .jisc.ac.uk/rd/projects/institution-as-e-textbook-publisher. [Accessed 14 April 2018].

Johnson, Rob, Watkinson, Anthony, & Mabe, Michael. (2018). *The STM Report An overview of scientific and scholarly publishing*. [ONLINE] Available at: www.stm-assoc.org/2018_10_04_STM_Report_2018.pdf. [Accessed 11 October 2018].

JS Group. (2017). *Aspire at York St John*. [ONLINE] Available at: https:// www.johnsmith.co.uk/yorksj/aspire-at-york-st-john. [Accessed 14 April 2018].

JS Group. (2018). *The Strategic Approach to Learning Resources*. [ONLINE] Available at: https://johnsmithgroup.co.uk/aspire-connect/. [Accessed 14 April 2018].

Kamenetz, Anya. (2016). *Pearson's Quest to Cover the Planet in Company-Run Schools*. [ONLINE] Available at: www.wired.com/2016/04/apec-schools/. [Accessed 14 April 2018].

Kane, Maryanne J. (2016). *Rapacious Testing Vendors Have No Place Assessing Potential Teachers*. [ONLINE] Available at: www.newsweek.com/rapacious-testing-vendors-no-place-assessing-teachers-513228. [Accessed 14 April 2018].

Kavanagh, Suzanne. (2015). *The Plymouth textbook project . . . paradise lost?* [ONLINE] Available at: http://blog.alpsp.org/2015/06/the-plymouth-textbook-project-paradise.html. [Accessed 14 April 2018].

Kidd, Terry T. & Keengwe, Jared. (2010). *Adult Learning in the Digital Age: Perspectives on Online Technologies and Outcomes*. Hershey: Information Science Reference.

Kim, Joshua. (2017). *A Q&A with the COO, Pep Carrera*. [ONLINE] Available at: www.insidehighered.com/digital-learning/blogs/why-VitalSource-wants-you-know-its-name. [Accessed 14 April 2018].

Knowledge Unlatched. (2018). *Making Open Access Work*. [ONLINE] Available at: http://www.knowledgeunlatched.org/. [Accessed 14 April 2018].

Koch, James V. (2014). *An Economic Analysis of the Market for Textbooks: Current Conditions, New Developments and Policy Options, The Future of the Textbook, University of Georgia Center for Continuing Education*. [ONLINE] Available at: www.affordablelearninggeorgia.org/documents/Koch_Plenary1.pdf [Accessed 14 April 2018].

Kovač, Miha, Phillips, Angus, van der Weel, Adriaan, & Wischenbart, Rüdiger (2017) *Book Statistics What are they good for?* [ONLINE] Available at: www.internationalpublishers.org/images/global-publishing-statistics/2018/LOGOS_28–4_pp._7–17.pdf . [Accessed 11 October 2018].

La Librairie des Puf. (2018). *Hypokhâgnes Khâgnes: nos bibliographies pour les concours de l'ENS*. [ONLINE] Available at: www.puf.com/. [Accessed 14 April 2018].

Lake, Peter. (2016a). *Keynote: Changing Models: A Future Role for the University* Bookseller. Bangor. The Future Space of Bookselling Conference.

Lake, Peter. (2016b). The Role of Booksellers. In R. Lyons and S. Rayner, eds., *The Academic Book of the Future*, Basingstoke: Palgrave. Macmillan, pp. 92–97.

Lawson, Matthew. (2015). Free e-books for all: the Middlesex University Library experience. *SOCONUL Focus* 63, 21–23.

Lazzari, Zach. (2018). *The Average Profit Margin in Furniture*. [ONLINE] Available at: https://smallbusiness.chron.com/average-profit-margin-furniture-37917.html. [Accessed 14 April 2018].

Leeds Beckett Student Union. (2018). *Student Council Motion: No More Hidden Fees*. [ONLINE] Available at: www.leedsbeckettsu.co.uk/thes tudentvoice/student-council-motion-no-more-hidden-fees.   [Accessed 14 April 2018].

Leishman, Mary & Cox, Joe. (2018). *What do students see as value for money, Fees & Funding Students*. [ONLINE] Available at: https://wonkhe.com/blogs/what-do-students-see-as-value-for-money/. [Accessed 14 April 2018].

Littlejohns, Peter. (2016). *New academic bookshop to open in New Cross*. [ONLINE] Available at: www.eastlondonlines.co.uk/2016/08/new-academic-bookshop-to-open-in-new-cross/. [Accessed 14 April 2018].

Liu, Z. (2018). Whither the Book Retailing Industry in China: A Historical Reflection. *Publishing Research Quarterly* 34: 133.

Lovegrove, Sharmaine. (2018). *If you don't have a diverse workforce or product, sooner or later you won't exist*. [ONLINE] Available at: www .theguardian.com/books/2018/mar/18/sharmaine-lovegrove-if-you -dont-have-diverse-workforce-wont-exist-dialogue-books-interview. [Accessed 14 April 2018].

MacIntosh, Robert & O'Gorman, Kevin D. (2015). *Introducing Management in a Global Context*. [ONLINE] Available at: https://researchportal.hw.ac.uk /en/publications/introducing-management-in-a-global-context. [Accessed 14 April 2018].

Marylebone Books Ltd. (2017). *Student Support*. [ONLINE] Available at: www.westminster.ac.uk/study/current-students/support-and-facilities /university-bookshops. [Accessed 14 April 2018].

Matthews, David. (2018). Elsevier's profits swell to more than £900 million. [ONLINE] www.timeshighereducation.com/news/elseviers-profits-swell-more-ps900-million. [Accessed 11 October 2018].

McGraw-Hill Education. (2017a). *Custom Book Sales*. [ONLINE] Available at: www.slideshare.net/mpcairns/high-level-overview-of-the-publishing -industry-2017. [Accessed 14 April 2018].

McGraw-Hill Education. (2017b). *New Research: More than Half of College Students Prefer Classes That Use Digital Learning Technology*. [ONLINE] Available at: www.mheducation.com/news-media/press-releases/col lege-students-prefer-classes-digital-learning-technology.html. [Accessed 14 April 2018].

McGraw-Hill Education. (2017c). *Success for Less, from Day One*. [ONLINE] Available at: www.mheducation.com/highered/inclusive-access.html. [Accessed 14 April 2018].

McKenzie, Lindsay. (2017). *'Inclusive Access' Takes Off*. [ONLINE] Available at: www.insidehighered.com/news/2017/11/07/inclusive-access-takes-model-college-textbook-sales. [Accessed 14 April 2018].

McNeish, Joanne, Foster, Mary, Francescucci, Anthony, & West, Bettina. (2012). The Surprising Foil to Online Education: Why Students Won't Give Up Paper Textbooks. *Journal for Advancement of Marketing Education* Volume 20 Issue 3 Fall 2012.

Minsky, Carly. (2016). *10 thoughts academics have about their students: THE University Workplace Survey 2016*. [ONLINE] Available at: www

.timeshighereducation.com/student/news/10-thoughts-academics-have-about-their-students-university-workplace-survey-2016. [Accessed 14 April 2018].

Mitchell, Josh. (2014). *A Tough Lesson for College Textbook Publishers*. [ONLINE] Available at: www.wsj.com/articles/a-tough-lesson-for-college-textbook- publishers-1409182139. [Accessed 14 April 2018].

National Association of College Stores. (2017). *Student Watch™: Attitudes and Behaviors toward Course Materials 2016–2017* [ONLINE] Available at: www.nacs.org/advocacynewsmedia/StudentSpendingInfographics .aspx. [Accessed 14 April 2018].

Nicholas, David, Rowlands, Ian & Jamali, Hamid R. (2014). E-textbook use, information seeking behaviour and its impact: Case Study Business and Management. *Journal of Information Science*, 36 (2).

Nicora, Roberta. (2017). *Kortext awarded tender for the JISC Learning Analytics Purchasing Service for UK Universities*. [ONLINE] Available at: www .kortext.com/kortext-won-tender-for-the-jisc-learning-analytics. [Accessed 14 April 2018].

Nicora, Roberta. (2018). *New Kortext analytics dashboard features Kortext*. [ONLINE] Available at: www.kortext.com/new-kortext-analytics-dashboard-features. [Accessed 14 April 2018].

Nielsen Book. (2016). *Students' Information Sources in the Digital World 2015–16*. [ONLINE] Available at: www.nielsenbook.co.uk/uploads/ press/1Student%27s%20Information%20Sources%20in%20the% 20Digital%20World%202015–16.pdf. [Accessed 14 April 2018].

Office for Students. (2016). *What is the TEF?* [ONLINE] Available at: www.officeforstudents.org.uk/advice-and-guidance/teaching/what-is-the-tef/#collapse-77d6c7b7-f790-4aac-b91e-958ea42d5f9 f-0. [Accessed 18 May 2018].

Office for Students. (2017). *Research Excellence Framework 2021*. [ONLINE] Available at: www.ref.ac.uk/. [Accessed 14 April 2018].

Office for Students. (2018a). *New research shines spotlight on student perceptions of value for money*. [ONLINE] Available at: www.officeforstudents.org.uk /news-blog-and-events/news-and-blog/new-research-shines-spotlight -on-student-perceptions-of-value-for-money/. [Accessed 14 April 2018].

Office for Students. (2018b). *The National Student Survey (NSS)*. [ONLINE] Available at: www.thestudentsurvey.com/. [Accessed 5 June 2018].

Office for Students. (2018c). *Value for money: the student perspective Research commissioned by the Office for Students. Project led by a consortium of student's unions*. [ONLINE] Available at: https://studentsunionresearch .files.wordpress.com/2018/03/value-for-money-the-student-perspective-final-final-final.pdf. [Accessed 14 April 2018].

Onwuemezi, Natasha. (2018a). *Authors defend W H Smith after retailer named 'worst shop'*. [ONLINE] Available at: www.thebookseller.com /news/authors-call-wh-smith-criticism-snobbery-793706. [Accessed 14 April 2018].

Onwuemezi, Natasha. (2018b). *Portsmouth Blackwell's closes after 15 years*. [ONLINE] Available at: www.thebookseller.com/news/portsmouth-blackwells-closes-745091. [Accessed 14 April 2018].

Open Access Directory. (2018). *OA book business models at the Open Access Directory*. [ONLINE] Available at: http://oad.simmons.edu/oadwiki/ OA_book_business_models. [Accessed 14 April 2018].

Open Access Textbooks Project. (2018). *Open Access Textbooks: A FIPSE grant project . . . creating a model for open textbook implementation*. [ONLINE] Available at: www.openaccesstextbooks.org/. [Accessed 14 April 2018].

Oxford University Press. (2018). *Oxford University Press India*. [ONLINE] Available at: https://india.oup.com/about. [Accessed 14 April 2018].

Page, Benedicte. (2017). *Publishers challenge HEFCE over OA monograph plans*. [ONLINE] Available at: www.thebookseller.com/news/publish

ers-challenge-hefce-over-oa-monograph-plans-733611. [Accessed 14 April 2018].

Page, Benedicte. (2018a). *Angry publishers debate OA monographs at IPG*. [ONLINE] Available at: www.thebookseller.com/news/angry-publishers-debate-oa-monographs-ipg-747211. [Accessed 14 April 2018].

Page, Benedicte. (2018b). *OA requirement for monographs will 'benefit society'*, *says Hill*. [ONLINE] Available at: www.thebookseller.com /insight/oa-requirement-monographs-will-benefit-society-says-hill -747196. [Accessed 14 April 2018].

Pan, Yuanyuan. (2016). *Education in China, A Snaphot, Organisation for Economic Co-operation and Development* (OECD). [ONLINE] Available at: www.oecd.org/china/Education-in-China-a-snapshot.pdf. [Accessed 14 April 2018].

Pearson Publishing Ltd. (2017a). *Charting Equity in Higher Education*. [ONLINE] Available at: www.pearson.com/corporate/about-pearson /innovation/charting-equity.html. [Accessed 14 April 2018].

Pearson Publishing Ltd. (2017b). *Pearson, Results, Improving Lives Through Learning*. [ONLINE] Available at: www.pearsonmylabandmastering.com /global/educators/results/index.php. [Accessed 14 April 2018].

Pearson Publishing Ltd. (2018a). *Stock record for Paul Deitel Java How to Program Pearson India*. [ONLINE] Available at: www.pearsoned.co.in /web/books/9789332563292_Java-How-to-Program_Paul-J-Deitel.aspx accessed 20/05/18. [Accessed 14 April 2018].

Pearson Publishing Ltd. (2018b). *Stock record for Paul Deitel Java How to Program Pearson US*. [ONLINE] Available at: www.pearson.com/us/ higher-education/product/Deitel-Java-How-To-Program-Early-Objects -10th-Edition/9780133807806.html accessed 20/05/18. [Accessed 14 April 2018].

Pearson Publishing Ltd. (2018c). *Welcome New York Educators*. [ONLINE] Available at: www.pearsonschool.com/index.cfm?locator=PS22H5. [Accessed 14 April 2018].

Pidd, Helen. (2017). *University of Manchester to axe 171 staff amid Brexit concerns*. [ONLINE] Available at: www.theguardian.com/uk-news /2017/may/10/university-of-manchester-to-axe-171-staff-amid-brexit-concerns. [Accessed 14 April 2018].

Pinfield, S., Salter, J., & Bath, P. A. (2016). The 'total cost of publication' in a hybrid open-access environment: Institutional approaches to funding journal article-processing charges in combination with subscriptions. *Journal of the Association for Information Science and Technology*, 67 (7) 1751–1766.

Publishers Communication Group. (2017). *Library Budget Predictions for 2017*. [ONLINE] Available at: www.pcgplus.com/wp-content /uploads/2017/05/Library-Budget-Predictions-for-2017-public.pdf. [Accessed 14 April 2018].

Radical Open Access Collective. (2018). *About the Collective*. [ONLINE] Available at: http://radicaloa.disruptivemedia.org.uk/. [Accessed 14 April 2018].

Raths, David. (2018). *When Learning Analytics Violate Student Privacy Campus Technology*. [ONLINE] Available at: https://campustechnol ogy.com/articles/2018/05/02/when-learning-analytics-violate-student -privacy.aspx. [Accessed 14 April 2018].

Reisz, Matthew. (2017). *Heriot-Watt University blames Brexit for redundancies*. [ONLINE] Available at: www.timeshighereducation.com/news/heriot-watt-university-blames-brexit-for-redundancies. [Accessed 14 April 2018].

Research Libraries UK. (2013). *Fair Prices for Article Processing Charges (APCs) in Hybrid Journals*. [ONLINE] Available at: www.rluk.ac.uk/wp-content /uploads/2014/02/RLUK-stance-on-double-dipping-Final-November -2013.pdf. [Accessed 14 April 2018].

Rheingold, Jennifer. (2015). *Everybody hates Pearson.* [ONLINE] Available at: http://fortune.com/2015/01/21/everybody-hates-pearson/. [Accessed 14 April 2018].

Ruiz, Ángela. (2017). *Robles at the Mujere Con Ciencia.* [ONLINE] Available at: https://mujeresconciencia.com/2017/05/25/angela-ruiz-robles-1895–1975/. [Accessed 14 April 2018].

Sandler, Nathaniel. (2013). *Why Bookstores Don't Reflect Miami's Literary Health.* [ONLINE] Available at: http://wlrn.org/post/why-bookstores-dont-reflect-miamis-literary-health. [Accessed 14 April 2018].

Searchlight. (2017). *Cengage Learning offers textbooks on subscription service.* [ONLINE] Available at: www.searchlightcap.com/news/cengage-launches-first-of-its-kind-subscription-to-offer-unlimited-on-demand-an/. [Accessed 14 April 2018].

Shah, Dhawal. (2017). *By the Numbers: MOOCS in 2017.* [ONLINE] Available at: www.class-central.com/report/mooc-stats-2017/. [Accessed 14 April 2018].

Shapiro, James. (1997). *Yes, a Big Seller Can Have Footnotes.* [ONLINE] Available at: https://archive.nytimes.com/www.nytimes.com/books/97/06/15/bookend/bookend.html?scp=50&sq=oxford&st=cse. [Accessed 14 April 2018].

Shils, Edward. (1963). The Bookstore in America. *Daedalus* 62 no. 1 Winter, 92–104.

Singer, Lauren M., Alexander, Patricia A. (2016). Reading Across Mediums: Effects of Reading Digital and Print Texts on Comprehension and Calibration. *The Journal of Experimental Education*, 85:1.

Singer, Lauren M. & Alexander, Patricia A. (2017). *Students learn better from books than screens.* [ONLINE] Available at: www.weforum.org/agenda/2017/10/students-learn-better-from-books-than-screens-according-to-a-new-study. [Accessed 14 April 2018].

Smith, Adam. (2014). *The Empire Strikes Back, Research Fortnight*. [ONLINE] Available at: https://adamesmith.files.wordpress.com/2014/11/nov-2014-the-empire-strikes-back-alicia-wise-elsevier-profile.pdf. [Accessed 14 April 2018].

Soper, Taylor. (2016). *Amazon charges non-Prime members more at physical bookstores, hinting at new retail strategy*. [ONLINE] Available at: www.geekwire.com/2016/amazon-gives-prime-members-better-prices-physical-bookstores-hinting-new-retail-strategy/. [Accessed 14 April 2018].

Southern Universities Purchasing Consortium. (2017). SUPC Awards One of the Largest Value Global Book Agreements for HE Sector. [ONLINE] www.supc.ac.uk/news/news/item/supc-awards-one-of-the-largest-global-value-book-agreements-for-he-sector. [Accessed 11 October 2018].

Stewart, Rod. (2005). Browser to buyer, Amazon style. [ONLINE] Available at: www.thebookseller.com/feature/browser-buyer-amazon-style. [Accessed 11 October 2018].

Stop Counterfeit Books. (2017). *Large-Scale Campaign Launches Against Trafficking in Counterfeit Books on Online Marketplaces*. [ONLINE] Available at: http://stopcounterfeitbooks.com/news/. [Accessed 14 April 2018].

Strauss, Valerie. (2016). *Pearson's history of testing problems – a list*. [ONLINE] Available at: www.washingtonpost.com/news/answer-sheet/wp/2016/04/21/pearsons-history-of-testing-problems-a-list/. [Accessed 14 April 2018].

Strauss, Valerie. (2018). *Pearson conducts experiment on thousands of college students without their knowledge*. [ONLINE] Available at: www.washingtonpost.com/news/answer-sheet/wp/2018/04/23/pearson-conducts-experiment-on-thousands-of-college-students-without-their-knowledge/. [Accessed 14 April 2018].

Tan, Teri. (2017). *Printing in Hong Kong & China 2017: Retooling the Hong Kong and China Print Business*. [ONLINE] Available at: www .publishersweekly.com/pw/by-topic/industry-news/manufacturing/ article/74588-printing-in-hong-kong-china-2017-retooling-the-hong-kong-and-china-print-business.html. [Accessed 14 April 2018].

The Academic Book of the Future. (2015). *What is an Academic Book?* [ONLINE] Available at: https://academicbookfuture.org/2015/04/ 17/what-is-an-academic-book/. [Accessed 14 April 2018].

The Academic Book of the Future. (2016). *Project*. [ONLINE] Available at: https://academicbookfuture.org/. [Accessed 14 April 2018].

The Academic Professional and Specialist Group. (2013–7). Student feedback panels, The Academic Professional and Specialist Group Conference (Booksellers Association).

The Booksellers Association. (2014). UK Book Sales Source of Purchase – 2009–2014 (%). (2017). [ONLINE]. www.booksellers.org.uk /BookSellers/BizFormFiles/3432732c-4ae9-4173-bf21-38a48d1e32b8.pdf. [Accessed 11 October 2018].

The Booksellers Association. (2017). 2001–2005 UK book retail market shares (%). [ONLINE]. www.booksellers.org.uk/industry/display_re port.asp?id=490 [Accessed 11 October 2018].

The Publishers Association. (2017). *UK Publishing has record year up 7% to £4.8bn*. [ONLINE] Available at: www.publishers.org.uk/news/press-releases/2017/uk-publishing-has-record-year-up-7-to-48bn/. [Accessed 14 April 2018].

The World Bank. (2018). Population ages 0–14 (% of total). [ONLINE] https://data.worldbank.org/indicator/sp.pop.0014.to.zs. [Accessed 11 October 2018].

Thomson, Flora. (2018). *WHSmith voted worst shop on the high street*. [ONLINE] Available at: www.independent.co.uk/news/business/

whsmith-worst-high-street-shop-john-lewis-which-survey-a8372246
.html. [Accessed 14 April 2018].

Thrush-Denning, Darrell & Hawker, Jaki. (2016). Internal sales figures.

Trachtenberg, Jeffrey A. (2009). *Booksellers Ask Justice Department to Investigate War Over Pricing* [ONLINE] Available at: www.wsj.com /articles/SB10001424052748703816204574489891863465178. [Accessed 11 October 2018].

UK Council for International Student Affairs. (2018). *International student statistics: UK higher education.* [ONLINE] Available at: www.ukcisa.org .uk/Research–Policy/Statistics/International-student-statistics-UK-higher -education. [Accessed 14 April 2018].

United States Government. (2018). *The FY18 omnibus appropriation bill.* [ONLINE] Available at: www.gpo.gov/fdsys/pkg/CPRT- 115HPRT29374/pdf/CPRT-115HPRT29374.pdf. [Accessed 14 April 2018].

United States International Trade Commission. (2010). *China, Intellectual Property Infringement, Indigenous Innovation Policies, and Frameworks for Measuring the Effects on the US Economy.* [ONLINE] Available at: www .usitc.gov/publications/332/pub4199.pdf. [Accessed 14 April 2018].

University of Sheffield Modern Languages Teaching Centre. (2017). *Blackwell's University Bookshop Student Price Match Guarantee.* [ONLINE] Available at: http://mltc.dept.shef.ac.uk/index.php/2017/ 01/26/blackwells-university-bookshop-student-price-match-guarantee -2/. [Accessed 14 April 2018].

Universities and Colleges Admissions Service. (2018). *UCAS Undergraduate tuition fees and student loans 2018/19.* [ONLINE] Available at: www.ucas.com/ucas/undergraduate/finance-and-support /undergraduate-tuition-fees-and-student-loans. [Accessed 18 May 2018].

Universities UK. (2017). *Patterns and Trends in UK Higher Education 2017.* [ONLINE] Available at: www.universitiesuk.ac.uk/facts-and-stats

/data-and-analysis/Documents/patterns-and-trends-2017.pdf. [Accessed 14 April 2018].

University College London Press. (2018). *Redux Conference 2018*. [ONLINE] Available at: www.ucl.ac.uk/ucl-press/ucl-press-news/university-press-redux-conference-2018. [Accessed 14 August 2018].

University of Chester. (2017). *John Smith's Aspire Books Scheme*. [ONLINE] Available at: www.chester.ac.uk/aspire. [Accessed 14 April 2018].

University of Essex. (2016). *Online £630 per student: the cost of paper textbooks*. [ONLINE] Available at: https://online.essex.ac.uk/blog/630-per-student-the-cost-of-paper-textbooks/. [Accessed 14 April 2018].

University of Kent. (2017). *Student Price Match Guarantee at Blackwells Bookshop*. [ONLINE] Available at: https://blogs.kent.ac.uk/staff-student-news/2017/01/12/student-price-match-guarantee-at-blackwells-bookshop/. [Accessed 14 April 2018].

University of Nottingham. (2017). *Blackwell's price match guarantee on books*. [ONLINE] Available at: https://exchange.nottingham.ac.uk/blog/blackwells-price-match-guarantee-on-books/. [Accessed 14 April 2018].

University of Stanford. (2016). *Kirtsaeng v. John Wiley & Sons, Inc.* [ONLINE] Available at: https://fairuse.stanford.edu/case/kirtsaeng-v-john-wiley-sons-inc-2/. [Accessed 14 April 2018].

University of Westminster. (2015). *Apple iPad mobile learning project*. [ONLINE] Available at: www.westminster.ac.uk/about-us/faculties/science-and-technology/news/apple-ipad-mobile-learning-project. [Accessed 14 April 2018].

Utton, Michael A. (2010). Books Are Not Different After All: Observations on the Formal Ending of the Net Book Agreement in the UK. *International Journal of the Economics of Business*, 7:1, 115–126

VitalSource. (2018). *VitalSource*. [ONLINE] Available at: www.VitalSource.com/. [Accessed 14 April 2018].

Wainwright, Henry. (2005). *Stock and Margin Management, Guides to Practical Bookselling, Independent Bookseller's Forum*. [ONLINE] Available at: www.booksellers.org.uk/BookSellers/media/Booksellers/Stock-and-Margin-IBF.pdf. [Accessed 14 April 2018].

Walker, Gaelle. (2015). *Access all areas: Welcoming disabled customers*. [ONLINE] Available at: www.convenienccstorc.co.uk/advice/your-business/access-all-areas-welcoming-disabled-customers/524281.article. [Accessed 14 April 2018].

Warwick University Bookshop. (2018). *Warwick University Bookshop*. [ONLINE] Available at: www.warwickbooks.com/default.asp. [Accessed 14 April 2018].

Waugh, Paul. (2018). *May Opens Way For Students To Be Excluded From Tory Immigration Target*. [ONLINE] Available at: www.huffingtonpost.co.uk/entry/theresa-may-paves-way-for-students-to-be-excluded-from-the-infamous-tory-immigration-target-commons-vote-due_uk_5a74b522e4b0905433b3f9c8. [Accessed 14 April 2018].

Wiley, Deborah E. (1996). *Collapse of the U.K.'s, Net Book Agreement, To Our Authors*. [ONLINE] Available at: www.wiley.com/legacy/authors/to/TOA2/cllps.html. [Accessed 14 April 2018].

Williams, Christopher. (2015). *Pearson woes deepen over UK ebook price row*. [ONLINE] Available at: www.telegraph.co.uk/finance/newsbysector/mediatechnologyandtelecoms/media/12048339/Pearson-woes-deepen-over-UK-ebook-price-row.html. [Accessed 14 April 2018].

Williams, Mark. (2017). *Global book market valued at $143bn*. [ONLINE] Available at: https://thenewpublishingstandard.com/global-book-market-valued-at-143bn/. [Accessed 11 October 2018].

Williams, Mark. (2018). *African publishers pay the price for putting all their eggs in one basket*. [ONLINE] https://thenewpublishingstandard.com/african-publishers-pay-price-putting-eggs-one-basket/.

Wilson-Higgins, Suzanne. (2017). *The Impact of Print-On-Demand on Academic Books*. Cambridge: Chandos Publishing.

Wischenbart, Rüdiger. (2018). *BookMap 2015–16*. [ONLINE] Available at: www.wischenbart.com/page-59#a_global_bookmap_in_smart_numbers %3A_the_new_collaborative_effort_on_publishing_statistics. [Accessed 14 April 2018].

Wolff-Eisenberg, Christine, Rod, Alisa B., & Schonfeld, Roger C. (2015) *UK Survey of Academics 2015 Ithaka S+R, Jisc, RLUK 2016*. [ONLINE] Available at: www.sr.ithaka.org/publications/uk-survey-of-academics -2015/. [Accessed 14 April 2018].

Wood, Heloise. (2017). *John Smiths adds York St John to its Aspire scheme*. [ONLINE] Available at: www.thebookseller.com/news/york-st-john-adopts-aspire-bursary-js-group-496166. [Accessed 14 April 2018].

Wood, Zoe. (2018). *Waterstones' annual profits jump 80% as buyers loom*. [ONLINE] Available at: www.theguardian.com/books/2018/jan/18/ waterstones-annual-profits-jump-80-percent-books-sale. [Accessed 14 April 2018].

XanEdu. (2018). *Simple solutions for tomorrow's learning*. [ONLINE] Available at: www.xanedu.com/. [Accessed 14 April 2018].

Cambridge Elements

Publishing and Book Culture

SERIES EDITOR
Samantha Rayner
University College London

Samantha Rayner is a Reader in UCL's Department of Information Studies. She is also Director of UCL's Centre for Publishing, co-Director of the Bloomsbury CHAPTER (Communication History, Authorship, Publishing, Textual Editing and Reading) and co-editor of the Academic Book of the Future BOOC (Book as Open Online Content) with UCL Press.

ASSOCIATE EDITOR
Rebecca Lyons
University of Bristol

Rebecca Lyons is a Teaching Fellow at the University of Bristol. She is also co-editor of the experimental BOOC (Book as Open Online Content) at UCL Press. She teaches and researches book and reading history, particularly female owners and readers of Arthurian literature in fifteenth- and sixteenth-century England, and also has research interests in digital academic publishing.

ABOUT THE SERIES

This series aims to fill the demand for easily accessible, quality texts available for teaching and research in the diverse and dynamic fields of Publishing and Book Culture. Rigorously researched and peer-reviewed Elements will be published under themes, or 'Gatherings'. These Elements should be the first check point for researchers or students working on that area of publishing and book trade history and practice: we hope that, situated so logically at Cambridge University Press, where academic publishing in the UK began, it will develop to create an unrivalled space where these histories and practices can be investigated and preserved.

Cambridge Elements

Publishing and Book Culture
Bookshops and Bookselling

Gathering Editor: Eben Muse

Eben Muse is Senior Lecturer in Digital Media at Bangor University and co-Director of the Stephen Colclough Centre for the History and Culture of the Book. He studies the impact of digital technologies on the cultural and commercial space of bookselling, and he is part-owner of a used bookstore in the United States.

Elements in the Gathering

Digital Authorship: Publishing in an Attention Economy
Lyle Skains
Capital Letters: The Economics of Academic Bookselling
J. M. Hawker

Printed in the United States
By Bookmasters